Brooke Foss Westcott

**The Paragraph Psalter**

Arranged for the Use of Choirs

Brooke Foss Westcott

**The Paragraph Psalter**
*Arranged for the Use of Choirs*

ISBN/EAN: 9783337296650

Printed in Europe, USA, Canada, Australia, Japan

Cover: Foto ©Thomas Meinert / pixelio.de

More available books at **www.hansebooks.com**

# THE

# PARAGRAPH PSALTER

## Arranged for the use of Choirs

BY

## BROOKE FOSS WESTCOTT, D.D., D.C.L.

BISHOP OF DURHAM;
SOMETIME CANON OF PETERBOROUGH.

**STEREOTYPED EDITION.**

Cambridge:
AT THE UNIVERSITY PRESS.
1895

# PREFACE.

DURING the last few years great care has been successfully bestowed upon the pointing of the Psalter, so as to ensure an intelligent musical rendering of each clause of the separate verses; but, as far as I am aware, no attempt has been made to exhibit the general structure of the Psalms in such a manner as to suggest the variety of musical treatment which is required in different Psalms and in different parts of the same Psalms for their true interpretation. The present arrangement, which has been made and tested during the last six years of my work at Peterborough, is an endeavour to obtain this object, or at least to indicate what must be aimed at, as far as I can judge, in order that the chanting of the Psalms may contribute in the highest degree to the edifying of the Choir and of the Congregation.

It is evident upon the least reflection that no one uniform method of chanting can be applicable to the whole Psalter. Sometimes the verses are separately complete; sometimes they are arranged in couplets, sometimes in triplets; sometimes they are grouped in unequal but corresponding masses.

*a*

In most cases the verses consist of two members, but not unfrequently they consist of three or four. If therefore the Psalms are sung antiphonally on one method in single verses, or in pairs of verses, or in half verses, the sense must constantly be sacrificed; and the Music instead of illuminating the thought will fatally obscure it.

Thus, for example, the second Psalm consists of four triplets, which offer remarkable internal correspondences. The teaching of the Psalm is wholly destroyed if the separate unity of these four stanzas is not clearly marked in chanting. There are cases again when the form of the composition is changed in its course. Thus in the nineteenth Psalm there is an abrupt transition from a triple to a double structure. The glory of God in the heavens is portrayed in two stanzas of three verses each: His glory in the Law, and man's consequent prayer, in two stanzas of four verses each. The simplest music which accentuates this form of composition necessarily directs the attention of the hearer to the progress of thought with which it corresponds. If no clear change of rendering meets the change of structure, the idea probably remains hidden. In the twenty-fourth Psalm, to take an illustration of a different kind, the question and answer in *vv.* 8, 10 ought clearly to be separated. There are also obvious changes of feeling, from confidence to prayer, from prayer to thanksgiving, and even alternations of feeling in the same Psalm, which call for musical recognition.

I have striven therefore, after long and repeated study, to mark the main divisions of the Psalms, and by very brief marginal notes to characterize them. The sharpest divisions are distinguished by a space and a dash (*e.g.* Ps. ii) : divisions more or less clear by a broader or narrower space (*e.g.* Ps. i and Ps. iii). In making them I have carefully weighed conflicting views. In some cases variations in my own judgment from time to time shew that the conclusion reached is uncertain ; but in the majority of Psalms the same outline of structure is recognised by a general consent of commentators, and cannot fail to approve itself to the reader.

It happens sometimes that the conjunctions which have been introduced in the Prayer-book Version mar the sequence of thought (i, 7, '*But* the Lord' in place of '*For* the Lord'; viii, 3, '*For I will*' in place of '*When I*'). These inaccuracies have necessarily been disregarded.

One important feature of many Psalms in relation to their musical rendering is the recurrence of 'refrains.' These are sometimes simple (Pss. viii, xlii f, xlix, lvii, lxii, lxvii, lxxx, lxxxvii, xcix, cxv, cxvi, cxxxvi), sometimes double (Pss. xxiv, lix, cvii), and sometimes complicated (cxviii). In all cases they require to be marked in some way so as to bring out plainly the character of the composition. In respect to these again the irregular freedom of the English version injures in several cases the perfect symmetry of the original. Thus in Ps. xlix, 12, the additional clause taken from *v.* 13 destroys the perfect correspondence with *v.* 20; in cxvi, 13

(parallel to 16*a*), the words *unto the Lord* are omitted
without authority, and *now* has the same claim to appear
in *v.* 16 as in *v.* 13; in cxlii, 6, 14, cxliii, 5, there are three
distinct renderings of one phrase (see also lix, 6, 14; cxviii,
1, 29; 10 ff. &c.).

The *Gloria* at the close of each Psalm must be regarded
as one uniform refrain. In many cases (*e. g.* Pss. lxxxviii,
cxlii f.) it ought to be rendered by a distinct chant, that
so the voice of praise may be clearly heard after the sad-
dest utterances. Sometimes it can be made in this way to
bind together a group of Psalms in a greater unity. Sometimes (as in Ps. cxix) it will mark by its measured recurrence successive breaks in the development of one idea.

In this connexion it may be noticed that the first four
of the five Books into which the Hebrew Psalter is divided
are closed by a special Doxology (Ps. xli, 13; lxxii, 18 f;
lxxxix, 50*b*; cvi, 46). These Doxologies form no part
of the Psalms to which they are appended, and should be
treated distinctly. As they stand at present, the Doxology in
Ps. xli wholly mars the structure of the Psalm; and that
in Ps. lxxxix mars the sense. The last Psalm is a grand
Doxology to the whole Psalter.

The 'refrains' and doxologies are printed in italics.

It has not seemed desirable to introduce into the text the
enigmatic word *Selah*. The term indeed appears to mark
some change in the original musical accompaniment,—perhaps
a passage for the instruments alone,—but its interpretation

is most uncertain, and an examination of the passages in which
it occurs leads to no positive result as to its general import.
It is found at the close of the following verses in the Psalter,
according to the numbering of the Prayer Book :

Ps. iii, 2, 4, 8.

„ iv, 2, 4.

„ vii, 5.

„ ix, 16 (Higgaion Selah), 20.

„ xx, 3.

„ xxi, 2.

„ xxiv, 6, 10.

„ xxxii, 4, 6, 8.

„ xxxix, 6, 12.

„ xliv, 9.

„ xlvi, 3, 7, 11.

„ xlvii, 4.

„ xlviii, 7.

„ xlix, 13, 15.

„ l, 6.

„ lii, 4, 6.

„ liv, 3.

„ lv, 7 (20 after *down*).

„ lvii, 3, 6.

„ lix, 5, 13.

Ps. lx, 4.

„ lxi, 4.

„ lxii, 4, 8.

„ lxvi, 3, 6, 13.

„ lxvii, 1, 4.

„ lxviii, 7, 19, 32.

„ lxxv, 4.

„ lxxvi, 3, 9.

„ lxxvii, 3, 9, 15.

„ lxxxi, 8.

„ lxxxii, 2.

„ lxxxiii, 8.

„ lxxxiv, 4, 8.

„ lxxxv, 2.

„ lxxxvii, 2, 6.

„ lxxxviii, 6, 10.

„ lxxxix, 4, 37, 44, 46.

„ cxl, 3, 5, 8.

„ cxliii, 6.

In the Psalter of 1549 (printed by H. Powell for E.
Whitchurch) the first *Sela* is printed with the comprehensive
note: 'Sela is as much to say as always, continually, for euer,
'forsoith, verely, a lifting up of the voice, or to make a
'pause, and earnestly to consydre and to ponder the sentence.'
It occurs again xxi, 2; xxxii, 6, 8; xxxix, 6 (mg.) 12; xliv, 9

(mg.); xlvi, 3, 11; xlvii, 4; xlviii, 7; xlix, 13, 15 (mg.) &c.
The occurrence, it will be seen, is quite irregular, but it would
justify the introduction of the term systematically if it were
otherwise desired.   It should however be added that I have
not observed the term in any other early Psalter (*e. g.*
Grafton 1549, Worcester 1549, Whitchurch 1552 (?), Jugge
and Cawood 1560, Barker 1590).

The verse-division of the Psalms in the Prayer Book
offers many difficulties in the way of their musical rendering.
This differs considerably from the division in the Hebrew
text, which is followed in the Bible Version.   Where the
Prayer Book division seriously obscured the structure of the
Psalms, I have ventured to alter it (*e. g.* i, 3 f; iv, 6 f; v, 9 f;
vii, 9 f; xvi, 4 f; xix, 14 f; xlviii, 2; lxiii, 1 f; lxxi, 1, 9; lxxviii,
38 f; xcii, 7; xcviii, 1 f; cxvi, 13, 16; cxxxix, 1.

In other cases I have not thought it well to disturb the
existing arrangement (*e. g.* x, 9 f; xi, 4 f; xv, 5 ff; xviii, 1,
43; xxii, 29 f; xxvii, 6 f, 10 f; xxviii, 14 f; xxx, 6 f, 9 f;
xxxi, 2 f; xxxix, 13 f; xliv, 21; xciii, 1 f; cv, 34; cxx, 3),
though it might have been better to restore the division of
lxxiii, 12, and to conform cviii, 8, 9 to the parallel lx, 7, 8.

The version has other faults of this kind which lie be-
yond any immediate remedy.   The translation of Ps. xxix,
for example, offers a striking instance of the destruction of
that symmetry of composition which it is one of the natural
aims of music to interpret.   In *v.* 1 the introduction of the
false duplicate rendering *bring young rams unto the Lord,*

destroys the perfect correspondence between the first two and the last two verses, with the fourfold repetition of the sacred Name.  Again in *v.* 3 the rendering, *it is the Lord that commandeth the waters*, for *the voice of the Lord is upon the waters*, entirely hides the first enunciation of the subject ; and the transference of the third member of the verse (*it is the Lord that ruleth the sea*) to the beginning of *v.* 4 is ruinous to the symmetry of both verses (see also xiv, 11, and lii, 7, 8).

The Prayer-book Psalter is indeed practically a ‘survival’ of our first English Bible.  It is described in the Preface as following ‘the translation of the great English Bible, set forth and used in the time of King Henry the Eighth and Edward the Sixth.’  More exactly, it is, I believe, a reproduction, not critically precise, of the last revision of this Bible (Nov. 1540[1]).  The ‘Great Bible’ (1539-1540) was a revision by Coverdale of Matthew’s Bible (1537), in which the Psalter was taken from Coverdale’s own translation of 1535.  The merits of this version, which render it ‘smoother and more easy to sing,’ caused it to be retained in 1662, when the other portions of Scripture used in Divine service were generally directed to be taken from the Revision of King James.  These merits belong to all the work of Coverdale, an exquisite rhythm, a graceful freedom of rendering, and an endeavour to represent the spirit as well

---

[1] The strange typographical error in Ps. lxviii, 4, *yea* for *Jah* (*Ja*, April 1540), is corrected.

as the letter of the original. But at the same time the
translation, which was very powerfully influenced by the
Zurich German Bible, by the Latin Version of Münster, and
by the Vulgate, is disfigured by many inaccuracies, and by
some interpolations from the current and familiar Latin
Vulgate.

In all the editions of the Great Bible which I have ex-
amined, these interpolations from the Latin are distinctly
marked by difference of type or by brackets according to
Coverdale's expressed purpose. They are also partially
distinguished in the Earliest Psalters[1] 'pointed for use in
Churches' (Powell for Whitchurch, Grafton [August], and
Worcester [September] 1549). But the round brackets which
are used to distinguish them are used even in the same
verses (*e.g.* Ps. ii, 12) for a different purpose, and nearly a
fourth, including the great interpolation in Ps. xiv (*vv.* 7—9),
are not marked at all. In the edition of 1564 by Jugge
and Cawood many more are neglected. In the edition of
Barker, 1590, a few only are marked (*e.g.* xiv, 2, 9; xviii, 49;
xxii, 1, 16, &c.) These facts shew how little critical care
was used in preparing the Psalter for use in Churches; but
it is clear that it would be in accordance with the purpose
of those who first printed it in this form to distinguish all
the additions to the Hebrew text[2].

---

[1] The Psalter of 1548 (printed by R. Car) is Coverdale's Version with very
slight variations: *e. g.* Ps. li, 1.

[2] As an example of the strange carelessness which prevailed, it may be
mentioned that Ps. xxxvii, 29 is printed *The* righteous *shall be punished* in Grafton,
Worcester (1549), Whitchurch (1552?), Jugge and Cawood (1564), Barker (1590).

The following is a list of the phrases which are marked in the Great Bible of April, 1540:

Ps. i, 5, *from the face of the earth.*

„ ii, 11, *unto him.*

„ „ 12, *right.*

„ iii, 2, (in) *his* (God).

„ iv, 8, *and oil.*

„ vii, 12, *strong and patient.*

„ xi, 5, *the poor.*

„ xiii, 6, *yea, I will...Highest.*

„ xiv, 2, *no not one.*

„ „ 5—7, *Their throat...their eyes.*

„ „ 9, *even where no fear was.*

„ xviii, 6, *holy.*

„ „ 49, *cruel.*

„ xix, 12, *my* (secret faults).

„ „ 14, *alway.*

„ xx, 9, *upon thee.*

„ xxii, 1, *look upon me.*

„ „ 16, *many* (dogs).

„ „ 31, *my* (seed).

„ „ 32, *the heavens.*

„ xxiii, 6, *thy* (loving-kindness).

„ xxiv, 4, *his neighbour.*

„ xxviii, 3, *neither destroy me.*

„ xxix, 1, *bring young rams unto the Lord.*

„ xxx, 7, *from me.*

„ xxxiii, 2, *unto him.*

„ „ 10, *and casteth...princes.*

„ xxxvi, 12, *all.*

Ps. xxxvii, 29, *The unrighteous shall be punished.*

„ xxxvii, 37, *his place.*

„ xxxviii, 16, *even mine enemies.*

„ xxxviii, 22, *God.*

„ xli, 1, *and needy.*

„ xlii, 12, *that trouble me.*

„ xlv, 10, *wrought...colours.*

„ „ 12, *God.*

„ xlvii, 6, (to) *our* (God).

„ xlviii, 3, *of the earth.*

„ l, 21, *wickedly.*

„ li, 1, *great.*

„ lv, 13, *peradventure.*

„ „ 20, *O Lord.*

„ lxv, 1, *in Jerusalem.*

„ lxvii, 1, *and be merciful unto us.*

„ lxxi, 7, *that I may sing of thy glory.*

„ lxxi. 18, *again.*

„ lxxiii, 13, *and said.*

„ „ 27, *in the gates...Sion.*

„ lxxvii, 13, (as) *our* (God).

„ lxxxv, 8, *concerning me.*

„ xc, 6, *dried up.*

„ xcv, 7, *the Lord.*

„ cviii. 1, *my heart is ready* (2°).

„ cxv, 9, *thou house of.*

„ cxviii, 2, *that he is gracious and.*

Ps. cxviii, 25, *me.*
  ,, cxix, 97, *Lord.*
  ,, cxx, 6, *unto them.*
  ,, cxxxii, 4, *neither...rest.*
  ,, cxxxiv, 1, *now.*
  ,,   ,, 2, *even in...God.*

Ps. cxxxvi, 27, *O give...ever.*
  ,, cxxxvii, 1, *thee O* (Sion).
  ,, cxlv, 15, *O Lord.*
  ,, cxlvii, 8, *and herb...man.*
  ,, cxlviii, 5, *he spake...made.*

It is not easy to see on what principle these additions were taken; for there are many other interpolations of the Vulgate Latin which are unnoticed though they have equal claims to recognition: *e.g.* Pss. v, 6, 10, 12; vii, 2; xviii, 35; xliv, 26; xlv, 4; xlviii, 11; lii, 6; lxvi, 3; lxviii, 32; cviii, 2; cxviii, 28; cxxxviii, 1; cxlvi, 13.

The Latin titles of the Psalms are, it may be added, the first words of the "Vulgate" version. This version having been made from the Greek (LXX) and not from the Hebrew, differs widely in many places from the original, so that the headings offer some remarkable variations from the English version, *e. g.* Pss. xxxvi, lxii, lxxiii, lxxx, lxxxiii, The common heading of Ps. cix (*Deus laudum*) is a mere error which I have ventured to correct.

This is not the place to enter further in detail into the mistakes of the Prayer-book Psalter. It is not perhaps too much to hope that the unquestionable errors of rendering and form may be dealt with by competent authority at no distant period. The question was prepared for Convocation in 1689, and it was proposed by the Commissioners 'to leave wholly to Convocation to consider and determine 'whether the amendment of the reading Psalms (as they

'are called) made by the Bishop of St Asaph [Lloyd] and
'Dr Kidder, or that of the Bible [1611] shall be inserted in
'the Prayer-book[1]'.

If such a revision were undertaken, it should be guided
by the spirit of Coverdale.    The precise and literal exact-
ness which is required in a version of Scripture for study
is not required in a version for use in public service.    For
such a purpose the main object must be to secure a plain
and rhythmical expression of the sense of the original, even
at the sacrifice of the letter ; and any one who will com-
pare the Prayer-book Psalter with the original will be able
to convince himself that the changes which are needed to
remove distinct mistakes could be made without injury to
its general character.

But even as it is the present text of the Prayer-book
Psalter preserves in the main the great features of the structure of the Psalms which Music has to illustrate.    In this
respect any musician who may accept the general princi-
ples of the present arrangement will determine for himself
how they can best be carried out in the particular circum-
stances with which he has to deal.    Every effect necessary
to give a true musical interpretation of the Psalms can be
secured by the simplest means, by the free change of the
melody, by the separate use of boys' and men's voices[2], by

[1] Cardwell, *Hist. of Conferences*, p. 431.
[2] 'The alternation between boys' and women's voices, when the Choir combines
'male and female singers, has a very striking effect.'  R. B.-B.

*b* 2

I need scarcely say that I could not have adequately tested the present arrangement of the Psalms without the hearty co-operation of our successive Precentors, the Rev. C. Daymond, Rev. W. F. Wilkinson, Rev. T. H. Vines, and Rev. S. Phillips, and from first to last of Dr H. Keeton, to whom I offer my warmest thanks. But above all I must acknowledge my debt to the Rev. R. Brown Borthwick, Vicar of All Saints, Scarborough, without whose advice and encouragement I should not have ventured to print the Psalter. While we were occupied with tentative 'paragraph' chanting at Peterborough, Mr Brown Borthwick sent me an account of a musical rendering of Ps. lxxviii by Dr Naylor, the organist of All Saints, which though far more elaborate in treatment was in principle identical with our own. This independent and striking confirmation of the method which I desired to see carried out, led to further communications with Mr Brown Borthwick, which shewed that he had formed the plan of a Psalter similar in its essential features to this, which has been completed with the assistance of his constant counsel. I should be unwilling to make Mr Brown Borthwick responsible for all the details in the execution of the plan, but I should be no less unwilling that he should not fully share any credit which may attach to the general conception; and every sheet has had the advantage of his criticism.

The pointing is, with few exceptions, taken by the permission of the Syndics of the Cambridge University Press from

'the Pointed Prayer Book,' with the addition of an asterisk
to mark one feature in the composition of some Psalms which
is generally overlooked. Most of the verses of the Psalms
consist, as has been already remarked, of two parallel members, and these are almost always correctly divided by the
central 'point' (yet see xv. 2); but a considerable number
of verses consist of three (see *e. g.* lxxvii, 16—19) or of four
members. These structural breaks are generally marked by
an asterisk; but in some cases the translation did not al-
low this method of notation (*c. g.* xxii, 14). A short pause
in the recitation before the asterisk will sufficiently indicate
the form of the composition.

If the book contributes in any degree to suggest new
modes of interpreting the Psalms in our public worship,
the labour which has been spent upon it will not have
been in vain. In our Cathedrals and great Churches the
Psalms are the centre of the service. They furnish splendid
opportunities for the consecration of the highest gifts of
musical genius and musical skill; and no nobler task can
be given to the religious artist than to interpret them in a
universal language. This is his proper office. The student
of Theology can only offer him some clue to their structure
and to their characteristic lessons in the hope that it may
be of service to him as he comes to offer his own gift in
Divine worship.

MINSTER PRECINCTS, PETERBOROUGH,
*August* 30, 1879.

# The Canticles and Hymns.

---

## At Morning Prayer.

## VENITE, EXULTEMUS DOMINO.

### Psalm xcv.

O COME, let us síng | unto·the | Lord : let us heartily rejóice in the | strength of | our sal-| vation. *A call to worship.*

2 Let us come before his présence with | thanks-| giving : and shéw ourselves | glad in | him with| psalms.

3 For the Lórd is a | great | God : and a gréat| King a-|bove all | gods. *The great-ness of God.*

4 In his hand are all the córners | of the | earth : and the stréngth of the | hills is | his | also.

5 The séa is his | and he | made it : and his hánds pre-|pared·the | dry | land.

6 O come, let us wórship and | fall | down : and knéel be-|fore the | Lord our | Maker. *A renew-ed call.*

7 For hé is the | Lord our | God : and we are the people of his pasture ánd the | sheep | of his | hand.

I

8 To-day if ye will hear his voice hárden | not Warnings against neglect.
your | hearts : as in the provocation and as in the
dáy of tempt-|ation | in the | wilderness ;

9 When your fáthers | tempted | me : próved | me
and | saw my | works.

10 Forty years long was I grieved with thís gener-|
ation·and | said : It is a people that do err in their
hearts, * fór they | have not | known my | ways.

11 Unto whom I swáre | in my | wrath : that they
shóuld not | enter | into·my | rest.

---

*Glory be to the Fáther, and | to the | Son : ánd | to
the | Holy | Ghost ;*

*As it was in the beginning, * is nów, and | ever|
shall be : wórld without | end. | A-|men.*

## ANTHEMS.

*(To be used on Easter Day instead of the* VENITE.)

C HRIST our passover is sácri-|ficed·for | us : Christ the true Pass-over.
thérefore | let us | keep the | feast.

2 Not with the old leaven, * nor with the léaven
of | malice·and | wickedness : but with the unleavened
bréad of sin-|ceri-|ty and | truth. 1 *Cor.* v. 7.

3 CHRIST being raised from the déad | dieth·no| In Christ Death and Life.
more : death hath no móre do-|minion | over | him.

4 For in that he díed, he díed unto | sin | once :
but in that he líveth, he | liveth | unto | God.

5 Likewise reckon ye also yourselves to be déad
indeed | unto | sin : but alive unto Gód through|
Jesus | Christ our | Lord. *Rom.* vi. 9.

6 CHRIST is rísen | from the | dead : and become In Christ the Resur- rection.
the fírst-|fruits of | them that | slept.

7 For sínce by | man came | death : by man came
also the résur-|rection | of the | dead.

8 For as in A'dam | all | die : even so in Christ
shall | all be | made a-|live.   I *Cor.* xv. 20.

---

*Glory be to the Fáther, and | to the | Son : ánd | to
the | Holy | Ghost;*

*As it was in the beginning,* * *is nów, and | ever|
shall be : wórld without | end. | A-|men.*

## HYMN.

*(To be used on the 20th of June instead of the* VENITE.)

O' | LORD our | Governour : how excellent ís God's gracious care of men.
thy | Name in | all the | world! *Psalm* viii. I.

2 Lord, what is man, that thou hast such respéct|
unto | him : or the son of man, thát thou | so re-|
gardest | him? *Psalm* cxliv. 3.

3 The merciful and gracious Lord hath so dóne
his | marvellous | works : that they óught to be | had|
in re-|membrance. *Psalm* cxi. 4.

4 O that men would therefore praise the Lórd|
for his | goodness : and declare the wonders that he
dóeth | for the | children·of | men. *Psalm* cvii. 8.

---

5 Behold, O Gód | our de-|fender : and look upón Prayers for the Queen.
the | face of | thine A-|nointed. *Psalm* lxxxiv. 9.

6 O hold thou up her góings | in thy | paths : thát
her | footsteps | slip | not. *Psalm* xvii. 5.

7 Grant the Quéen a | long | life : and make her

glád with the | joy | of thy | countenance. *Psalms* lxi. 6 and xxi. 6.

8 Let her dwéll before | thee for | ever : O prepare thy loving mercy and faíthfulness | that they | may pre-|serve her. *Psalm* lxi. 7.

9 In her tíme let the | righteous | flourish : and let peáce | be in | all our | borders. *Psalms* lxxii. 7 and cxlvii. 14.

10 As for her enemies, clóthe | them with | shame : but upon hersélf | let her | crown | flourish. *Psalm* cxxxii. 19.

11 Blessed be the Lord God, éven the | God of | Israel : which ónly | doeth | wondrous | things. *Psalm* lxxii. 18.   Thanks-giving to God.

12 And blessed be the Name of his Májes-|ty for | ever : and all the earth shall be filled with his Májesty. | Amen, | A-|men. *Psalm* lxxii. 19.

---

*Glory be to the Fáther, and | to the | Son : ánd | to the | Holy | Ghost;*

*As it was in the beginning,* * *is nów, and | ever| shall be : wórld without | end. | A-|men.*

## TE DEUM LAUDAMUS.

WE praíse | thee O | God : we acknówledge| thee to | be the | Lord.   The praise of God on

2 All the éarth doth | worship | thee : thé | Father| ever-|lasting.   earth and in heaven.

3 To thee all A'ngels | cry a-|loud : the Heávens, and | all the | Powers there-|in.

4 To thee Chérubin and | Seraph-|in : cón-|tinual-| ly do | cry,

5 Hóly | Holy | Holy **:** Lórd | God of | Saba-|oth ;

6 Heaven and earth are fúll of the | Majes-|ty **:** óf |
thy | Glo-|ry.

7 The glorious cómpany | of·the A-|postles **:**
práise | — | — | thee.

8 The goodly féllowship | of the | Prophets **:** práise|
— | — | thee.

9 The nóble | army·of | Martyrs **:** práise | — | —|
thee.

———————

10 The holy Chúrch throughout | all the | world **:** A confes-
dóth ac-|know-|ledge | thee ; sion of
Faith.

11 Thé | Fa-|ther **:** óf an | infinite | Majes-|ty ;

12 Thine hónour-|able | true **:** ánd | on-|—ly | Son;

13 A'lso the | Holy | Ghost **:** thé | Com-|fort-|er.

———————

14 Thóu art the | King of | Glory **:** O' | — | —|
Christ.

15 Thou art the éver-|lasting | Son **:** óf | —the|
Fa-|ther.

16 When thou tookest upón thee to de-|liver|
man **:** thou dídst not ab-|hor the | Virgin's | womb.

17 When thou hadst overcóme the | sharpness·of |
death **:** thou didst open the Kíngdom of | Heaven
to | all be-|lievers.

18 Thou sittest at the ríght | hand of | God **:** ín
the | Glory | of the | Father.

19 We beliéve that | thou shalt | come **:** tó | be|
our | Judge.

———————

20 We therefore práy thee | help thy | servants **:** Prayer
whom thou hast redeémed | with thy | precious| resting on
trust.
blood.

21 Make them to be númbered | with thy | Saints : ín | glory | ever-|lasting.

22 O Lórd | save thy | people : ánd | bless thine| herit-|age.

23 Góv- | — ern | them : ánd | lift them | up for| ever.

24 Dáy | by | day : wé | magni- | fy | thee ;

25 A'nd we | worship·thy | Name : éver | world with-|out | end.

26 Voúch-|safe O | Lord : to kéep us this | day with-|out | sin.

27 O Lórd have | mercy·up-|on us : háve | mer-| cy up-|on us.

28 O Lord let thy mércy | lighten·up- | on us : ás our | trust | is in | thee.

29 O Lord in thée | have I | trusted : lét me| never | be con-|founded.


## BENEDICITE, OMNIA OPERA.

O ALL ye Works of the Lórd | bless·ye the| Lord : práise him, and | magnify | him for | ever.   Call to universal praise

2 O ye Angels of the Lórd | bless·ye the | Lord : práise him, and | magnify | him for | ever.   from the unseen powers in Heaven above ;

3 O ye Heávens | bless·ye the | Lord : práise him, and | magnify | him for | ever.

4 O ye Waters that be above the Fírmament| bless·ye the | Lord : práise him, and | magnify | him for | ever.

5 O all ye Powers of the Lórd | bless·ye the | Lord :
práise him, and | magnify | him for | ever.


6 O ye Sun and Moón | bless·ye the | Lord : práise
him, and | magnify | him for | ever.

7 O ye Stars of Heáven | bless·ye the | Lord :
práise him, and | magnify | him for | ever.

8 O ye Showers and Déw | bless·ye the | Lord :
práise him, and | magnify | him for | ever.

9 O ye Winds of Gód | bless·ye the | Lord : práise
him, and | magnify | him for | ever.

10 O ye Fire and Héat | bless·ye the | Lord :
práise him, and | magnify | him for | ever.

11 O ye Winter and Súmmer | bless·ye the | Lord :
práise him, and | magnify | him for | ever.

12 O ye Dews and Frósts | bless·ye the | Lord :
práise him, and | magnify | him for | ever.

13 O ye Frost and Cóld | bless·ye the | Lord :
práise him, and | magnify | him for | ever.

14 O ye Ice and Snów | bless·ye the | Lord : práise
him, and | magnify | him for | ever.

15 O ye Nights and Dáys | bless·ye the | Lord :
práise him, and | magnify | him for | ever.

16 O ye Light and Dárkness | bless·ye the | Lord :
práise him, and | magnify | him for | ever.

17 O ye Lightnings and Clóuds | bless·ye the|
Lord : práise him, and | magnify | him for | ever.

*from the
visible
powers of
the Sky ;*


18 O let the Eárth | bless the | Lord : yea let it
práise him, and | magnify | him for | ever.

19 O ye Mountains and Hílls | bless·ye the | Lord :
práise him, and | magnify | him for | ever.

*from Earth
and the
manifold
Creatures
of the
earth ;*

20 O all ye Green Things upon the Eárth | bless·ye the | Lord : práise him, and | magnify | him for | ever.

21 O ye Wélls | bless·ye the | Lord : práise him, and | magnify | him for | ever.

22 O ye Seas and Flóods | bless·ye the | Lord : práise him, and | magnify | him for | ever.

23 O ye Whales, and all that move in the Wáters| bless·ye the | Lord : práise him, and | magnify | him for | ever.

24 O all ye Fowls of the Aír | bless·ye the | Lord : práise him, and | magnify | him for | ever.

25 O all ye Beasts and Cáttle | bless·ye the | Lord : práise him, and | magnify | him for | ever.

26 O ye Children of Mén | bless·ye the | Lord : práise him, and | magnify | him for | ever. _from Men in their various estates._

27 O let I'srael | bless the | Lord : práise him, and| magnify | him for | ever.

28 O ye Priests of the Lórd | bless·ye the | Lord : práise him, and | magnify | him for | ever.

29 O ye Servants of the Lórd | bless·ye the | Lord : práise him, and | magnify | him for | ever.

30 O ye Spirits and Souls of the Ríghteous | bless· ye the | Lord : práise him, and | magnify | him for| ever.

31 O ye holy and humble Men of héart | bless·ye the | Lord : práise him, and | magnify | him for | ever.

32 O Ananias, Azarias, and Mísael | bless·ye the| Lord : práise him, and | magnify | him for | ever.

---

_Glory be to the Fáther, and | to the | Son : and | to the | Holy | Ghost ;_

_As it was in the beginning, * is nów, and | ever| shall be : wórld without | end. | A-|men._

## BENEDICTUS.

### S. Luke i. 68.

BLESSED be the Lórd | God of | Israel : for he
hath vísited | and re-|deemed · his | people ;
  2 And hath raised up a míghty sal-|vation | for us :
in the hóuse | of his | servant | David ;

The ful-
filment of
old pro-
phecy.

  3 As he spake by the móuth of his | holy | Pro-
phets : which have beén | since the | world be-|gan ;
  4 That we should be sáved | from our | enemies :
and fróm the | hands of | all that | hate us ;

  5 To perform the mercy prómised | to our | fore-
fathers : ánd to re-|member · his | holy | Covenant ;

  6 To perform the oath which he swáre to our | fore-
father | Abraham : thát | he would | give | us ;

  7 That we being delivered out of the hánd | of our|
enemies : might sérve | him with-|out | fear ;
  8 In holiness and ríghteous-|ness be-|fore him : áll
the | days | of our | life.

———

  9 And thou Child shalt be called the Próphet | of
the | Highest : for thou shalt go before the face of the
Lórd | to pre-|pare his | ways ;
  10 To give knowledge of salvátion | unto · his|
people : fór the re-|mission | of their | sins,

The work
of the new
Elijah.

  11 Through the tender mércy | of our | God : where-|
by the day-spring fróm on | high hath | visited | us ;

12 To give light to them that sit in darkness * and in the | shadow·of | death : and to guide our féet| into·the | way of | peace.

*Glory be to the Fáther, and | to the | Son : ánd | to the | Holy | Ghost ;*

*As it was in the beginning * is nów, and | ever | shall be : wórld without | end. | A-|men.*

## JUBILATE DEO.

### PSALM C.

O BE joyful in the Lórd | all ye | lands : serve the Lord with gladness * and come befóre his | pre- sence | with a | song.

2 Be ye sure that the Lórd | he is | God : it is he that hath made us and not we ourselves * we are his people, ánd the | sheep of | his | pasture.

*A two-fold call and ground for wor-ship.*

3 O go your way into his gates with thanksgiving * and ínto his | courts with | praise : be thankful unto hím, and | speak good | of his | Name.

4 For the Lord is gracious * his mércy is | ever-| lasting : and his truth endureth from géner-|ation·to| gener-|ation.

*Glory be to the Fáther, | and·to the | Son : ánd | to the | Holy | Ghost ;*

*As it was in the beginning * is nów, and | ever | shall be : wórld without | end. | A-|men.*

## QUICUNQUE VULT.

WHOSOEVER will be | sav-ed : before all things it is necessary that he hold the Cátholick | Faith.

2 Which Faith except every one do keep whóle and unde-|filed : without doubt he shall pérish ever-| lastingly.

3 And the Catholick Fáith is | this : that we wor- ship one God in Trinity, * and Trínity in | Unity ;

4 Neither confóunding the | Per-sons : nor divíding the | Substance.

A confession of faith in the Holy Trinity.

5 For there is one Person of the Father, * anóther of the | Son : and another of the Hóly | Ghost.

6 But the Godhead of the Father, of the Son, and of the Holy Ghost, is áll | one : the Glory equal,* the Majesty có-e-|ternal.

7 Such as the Father is, * súch is the | Son : and such is the Hóly | Ghost.

8 The Father uncreate, * the Són uncre-|ate : and the Holy Ghóst uncre-|ate.

9 The Father incomprehensible, * the Són incom-pre-|hensi-ble : and the Holy Ghóst incompre-|hensible.

10 The Father eternal, * the Són e-|ter-nal : and the Holy Ghóst e-|ternal.

11 And yet they are not thrée e-|ter-nals : but óne e-|ternal.

12 As also there are not three incomprehensibles, * nor thrée uncre-|a-ted : but one uncreated, * and óne incompre-|hensible.

13 So likewise the Father is Almighty, * the Són Al-|might-y : and the Holy Ghóst Al-|mighty.

14 And yet they are not thrée Al-|might-ies : but óne Al-|mighty.

15 So the Father is God, * the Són is | God : and the Holy Ghóst is | God.

16 And yet they are not thrée | Gods : but óne| God.

17 So likewise the Father is Lord, * the Són | Lord : and the Holy Ghóst | Lord.

18 And yet not thrée | Lords : but óne | Lord.

19 For like as we are compelled by the Christian| veri-ty : to acknowledge every Person by Himself to be Gód and | Lord;

20 So are we forbidden by the Cátholick Re-|li-gion : to say, There be three Gods, * or thrée | Lords.

21 The Father is máde of | none : neither created nór be-|gotten.

22 The Son is of the Fáther a-|lone : not made, nor created * bút be-|gotten.

23 The Holy Ghost is of the Father and óf the| Son : neither made, nor created, nor begotten * bút pro-|ceeding.

24 So there is one Father, not three Fathers * one Son, not thrée | Sons : one Holy Ghost, not thrée Holy | Ghosts.

25 And in this Trinity none is afore or áfter | oth-er : none is greater or léss than an-|other;

26 But the whole three Persons are co-etérnal to-|geth-er : ánd co-|equal.

27 So that in all things, ás is a-|fore-said : the Unity in Trinity * and the Trinity in Unity ís to be| worshipped.

28 He therefore that wíll be | sav-ed : must thus thínk of the | Trinity.

29 Furthermore, it is necessary to everlásting sal-| va-tion : that he also believe rightly the Incarnation of our Lord Jésus | Christ.

30 For the right Faith is, that we beliéve and con-| fess : that our Lord Jesus Christ, the Son of God, is Gód and | Man;

31 God, of the Substance of the Father, begotten befóre the | worlds : and Man, of the Substance of his Mother, bórn in the | world.

32 Perfect God, and pérfect | Man : of a reasonable soul and human flésh sub-|sisting.

33 Equal to the Father, as toúching his | God-head : and inferior to the Father, as toúching his | Man-hood.

34 Who although he be Gód and | Man : yet he is not two, but óne | Christ.

35 One; not by conversion of the Gódhead into| flesh : but by taking of the Mánhood into | God;

36 One altogether * not by confúsion of | sub-stance : but by únity of | Person.

37 For as the reasonable soul and flesh is óne | man : so God and Man is óne | Christ;

A confes-sion of faith in the Incar-nation.

38 Who suffered for oúr sal-|vation : descended into hell, * rose again the third dáy from the| dead.

39 He ascended into heaven, * he sitteth on the right hand of the Father Gód Al-|might-y : from whence he shall come to judge the quíck and the| dead.

40 At whose coming all men shall rise agáin with their | bod-ies : and shall give account for their ówn| works.

41 And they that have done good shall go into lífe ever-|last-ing : and they that have done evil into everlásting | fire.

42 This is the Cátholick | Faith : which except a man believe faithfully, he cáńnot be | saved.

*Glory be to the Father,* and tó the | Son : and to the Hóly | Ghost;

*As it was in the beginning* is now, and éver | shall be : world without end * A'-|men.*

## At Evening Prayer.

## MAGNIFICAT.

### S. Luke i. 46.

MY soul doth mágni-|fy the | Lord : and my spi- rit háth re-|joiced·in | God my | Saviour.

2 For he hath regarded the lowliness of hís | hand-| maiden : 3 for behold from henceforth all gener-|ations· shall | call me | blessed

4 For he that is míghty hath | magnified | me : ánd| holy | is his | Name.

5 And his mércy is on | them that | fear him : throughóut | all | gener-|ations.

*Thanksgiving for God's special grace.*

6 He hath shewed stréngth | with his | arm : he hath scattered the proud in the imágin-|ation | of their| hearts.

7 He hath put down the míghty | from their | seat : and háth ex-|alted·the | humble·and | meek.

8 He hath filled the húngry with | good | things : and the rích he hath | sent | empty·a-|way.

9 He remembering his mercy hath hólpen his| servant | Israel : as he promised to our forefathers, A'braham | and his | seed for | ever.

*His judgments and faithfulness.*

*Glory be to the Fáther, and | to the | Son : ánd | to the | Holy | Ghost ;*

*As it was in the beginning \* is nów, and | ever| shall be : wórld without | end. | A-|men.*

## CANTATE DOMINO.

### Psalm xcviii.

O SING unto the Lord a new song,* for he hath
dóne | marvellous | things : 2 with his own right
hand, and with his holy arm, háth he | gotten·him-|
self the | victory.

God's
victory for
His
people.

3 The Lord declárcd | his sal-|vation : his righte-
ousness hath he openly shéwed in the | sight | of the|
heathen.

4 He hath remembered his mercy and truth, * tó-
ward the | house of | Israel : and all the ends of the
world * have séen the sal-|vation | of our | God.

5 Shew yourselves joyful unto the Lórd | all ye|
lands : síng, re-|joice and | give | thanks.

Let men
and

6  Praise the Lórd up-|on the | harp : sing to the
hárp with a | psalm of | thanks-|giving.

7 With trúmpets | also and | shawms : O shew your-
sclves jóyful be-|fore the | Lord the | King.

8 Let the sea make a noise,* and áll that | therein|
is : the round wórld, and | they that | dwell there-|in.

nature
praise
Him for
His judg-
ment.

9 Let the floods clap their hands,* and let the hills
be joyful togéther be-|fore the | Lord : fór he | cometh
·to | judge the | earth.

10 With righteousness sháll he | judge the | world :
ánd the | people | with | equity.

*Glory be to the Fáther, and | to the | Son : ánd | to
the | Holy | Ghost ;*

*As it was in the beginning* is nów, and | ever | shall
be : wórld without | end. | A-|men.*

## NUNC DIMITTIS.

### S. Luke ii. 29.

LORD, now lettest thou thy sérvant de-|part in| peace : ác-|cording | to thy | word.

2 Fór mine | eyes have | seen : thý | — sal-|va-| tion,

3 Which thou | hast pre-|pared : befóre the | face of | all | people;

4 To be a líght to | lighten·the | Gentiles : and to be the glóry | of thy | people | Israel.

*Glory be to the Fáther, and | to the | Son : ánd | to the | Holy | Ghost ;*

*As it was in the beginning * is nów, and | ever | shall be : wórld without | end. | A-|men.*

Perfect rest in the sight of

God's universal purpose of love.

## DEUS MISEREATUR.

### Psalm lxvii.

GOD be merciful únto | us and | bless us : and shew us the light of his countenance * ánd be| merciful | unto | us :

2 That thy way may be knówn up-|on | earth : thy sáving | health a-|mong all | nations.

3 Let the people práise | thee O | God : yeá let | all the | people | praise thee.

Prayer and praise for blessings future and past.

3

4 O let the nations rejóice | and be | glad : for thou shalt judge the folk righteously * and góvern the | na- tions·up-|on | earth.

5 Let the people práise | thee O | God : yeá let| all the | people | praise thee.

6 Then shall the éarth bring | forth her | increase : and God, even our own Gód, shall | give | us his| blessing.

7 Gód | shall | bless us : and all the énds of the| world shall | fear | him.

*Glory be to the Fáther, and | to the | Son : ánd | to the | Holy | Ghost ;*
*As it was in the beginning * is nów, and | ever | shall be : wórld without | end. | A-|men.*

# The Psalms of David.

## Morning Prayer.

### PSALM I. *Beatus vir, qui non abiit.*

BLESSED is the man that hath not walked in the counsel of the ungodly, * nor stóod in the| way of | sinners : and hath not sát in the | seat | of the | scornful. The blessedness of the righteous

2 But his delight is in the láw | of the | Lord : and in his law will he éxercise him-|self | day and| night.

3 And he shall be like a tree planted by the water-side, * that will bring forth his frúit in | due | season : 4 His leaf also shall not wither ;*and look, whatsoéver he | doeth | it shall | prosper.

5 As for the ungodly, it ís not | so with | them : but they are like the chaff, * which the wind scat-tereth awáy from the | face | of the | earth. contrasted with the fate of the ungodly.

6 Therefore the ungodly shall not be able to stánd | in the | judgement : neither the sinners in the cón-greg-|ation | of the | righteous.

7 But the Lord knoweth the wáy | of the | right-eous : and the wáy | of · the un-|godly · shall | perish.

3—2

### PSALM II. *Quare fremuerunt gentes?*

WHY do the heathen so fúriously | rage to-| gether : and why do the péople im-|agine· a | vain | thing ?

*The rebellion of the nations.*

2 The kings of the earth stand up, * and the rúlers take | counsel · to-|gether : against the Lórd, and a-|gainst | his an-|ointed.

3 "Let us bréak their | bonds a-|sunder : and cást a-|way their | cords | from us."

———————

4 He that dwelleth in heaven shall láugh | them to | scorn : the Lórd shall | have them | in de-|rision.

*The answer of Jehovah.*

5 Then shall he spéak unto them | in his | wrath : and véx them | in his | sore dis-|pleasure.

6 " Yét have I | set my | King : upón my | holy | hill of | Sion."

———————

7 I will preach the law, * whereof the Lord hath sáid | unto | me : Thou art my Son, * this dáy have | I be-|gotten | thee.

*The commission of the Divine King.*

8 Desire of me, * and I shall give thee the héathen for | thine in-|heritance : and the utmost párts of the | earth for | thy pos-|session.

9 Thou shalt brúise them with a | rod of | iron : and break them in píeces | like a | potter's | vessel.

———————

10 Be wise now thérefore, | O ye | kings : be learned, yé that are | judges | of the | earth.

*The counsel of submission.*

11 Sérve the | Lord in | fear : and rejóice | unto | him with | reverence.

12 Kiss the Son lest he be angry, and so ye pérish from the | right | way : if his wrath be kindled, yea but a little, * blessed are all théy that | put their | trust in | him.

## PSALM III.    *Domine, quid multiplicati?*

LORD, how are they incréased that | trouble | me : mány are | they that | rise a-|gainst me.

Many enemies.

2 Many one there be that sáy | of my | soul : There is no hélp | for him | in his | God.

3 But thou O Lórd, art | my de-|fender : thou art my worship, and the lífter | up of | my | head.

One defender.

4 I did call upon the Lórd | with my | voice : and he héard me | out of·his | holy | hill.

5 I laid me down and slept, * and róse | up a-|gain : fór the | Lord sus-|tained | me.

Sure trust.

6 I will not be afraid for ten thóusands | of the| people : that have sét themselves a-|gainst me | round a-|bout.

7 Up Lord, and hélp me | O my | God : for thou smitest all mine enemies upon the cheek-bone ; * thou hast bróken the | teeth of | the un-|godly.

Righteous judgment.

8 Salvation belóngeth | unto·the | Lord : and thy bléssing | is up-|on thy | people.

## PSALM IV.    *Cum invocarem.*

HEAR me when I call, O Gód | of my | righte-ousness : thou hast set me at liberty when I was in trouble; * have mercy upón me and | hearken| unto·my | prayer.

2 O ye sons of men, how lóng will ye blas-|pheme
mine | honour : and have such pleasure in vánity and|
seek | after | leasing ?

3 Know this also, that the Lord hath chosen to
himself the mán | that is | godly : when I cáll upon
the | Lord, | he will | hear me.

4 Stánd in | awe, and | sin not : commune with
your own heart, and ín your | chamber, | and be|
still.

5 Offer the sácri-|fice of | righteousness : * and put
your | trust | in the | Lord.

6 There be many that say, * Who will shéw us | any|
good : 7 Lord, lift thou up the líght of thy | counten-|
ance up-|on us.

8 Thou hast put gládness | in my | heart : since the
time that their córn, and | wine, and | oil, in-|creased.


9 I will lay me down in péace, and | take my | rest:
for it is thou Lord ónly that | makest·me | dwell in|
safety.


## PSALM V.   *Verba mea auribus.*

PÓNDER my | words, O | Lord : cón-|sider·my|
    medit-|ation.

2 O hearken thou unto the voice of my calling,
my Kíng, | and my | God : for unto thée | will I|
make my | prayer.


3 My voice shalt thou héar be-|times, O | Lord :
early in the morning will I direct my prayer unto
thée, | and will | look | up.

4 For thou art the God that hást no | pleasure·in|
wickedness : neither shall ány | evil | dwell with|
thee.

5 Such as be foolish shall not stánd | in thy | sight:
for thou hátest all | them that | work | vanity.

6 Thou shalt destroy thém that | speak | leasing :
the Lord will abhor both the blóod-thirsty | and de-|
ceitful | man.

7 But as for me I will come into thine house, even
upon the múltitude | of thy | mercy : and in thy fear
will I wórship | toward·thy | holy | temple.


8 Lead me O Lord in thy righteousness, becáuse| His prayer
of mine | enemies : make thy wáy | plain be-|fore for right-
my | face.                                              eous judg-
                                                        ment.
9 For there is no faithfulness in his mouth ; * their
inward párts are | very | wickedness : 10 Their throat
is an open sepulchre ; * théy | flatter | with their|
tongue.

11 Destroy thou them O God ; * let them perish
through their ówn im-|agin-|ations : cast them out in
the multitude of their ungodliness ; * for they háve re-|
belled·a-|gainst | thee.

12 And let all them that put their trúst in | thee
re-|joice : they shall ever be giving of thanks because
thou defendest them ; * they that love thy Náme | shall
be | joyful·in | thee ;

13 For thou Lord wilt give thy bléssing | unto·the|
righteous : and with thy favourable kindness wilt thóu
de-|fend him | as·with a | shield.

## Ebening Prayer.

### PSALM VI. *Domine, ne in furore.*

O LORD rebuke me nót in thine | indig-|nation :    Prayer in affliction.
néither | chasten me in | thy dis-|pleasure.

2 Have mercy upon me O Lórd, for | I am | weak :
O Lord héal me, | for my | bones are | vexed.

3 My sóul also is | sore | troubled : but Lord how
lóng | wilt thou | punish | me ?

4 Turn thee O Lórd, and de-|liver·my | soul : O    Prayer yet more urgent.
sáve me | for thy | mercy's | sake.

5 For in death nó man re-|membereth | thee : and
who will gíve thee | thanks | in the | pit ?

6 I am weary of my groaning ; * every níght wash|
I my | bed : and wáter my | couch | with my | tears.

7 My beauty is góne for | very | trouble : and worn
awáy be-|cause of | all mine | enemies.

8 Away from me, all yé that | work | vanity : for    Thanksgiving for prayer heard.
the Lord hath héard the | voice | of my | weeping.

9 The Lord hath héard | my pet-|ition : the Lórd|
will re-|ceive my | prayer.

10 All mine enemies shall be confóunded and | sore|
vexed : they shall be turned báck, and | put to | shame|
suddenly.

### PSALM VII. *Domine, Deus meus.*

O LORD my God, in thée have I | put my | trust :    The appeal of the innocent to God.
save me from all them that pérsecute me, | and
de-|liver | me ;

2 Lest he devour my soul like a líon and | tear it ·
in | pieces : whíle | there is | none to | help.

3 O Lord my God, if I have dóne | any · such | thing :
or if there bé any | wickedness | in my | hands ;

4 If I have rewarded evil unto him that déalt|
friendly | with me : yea I have delivered him that
withóut any | cause | is mine | enemy ;

5 Then let mine enemy pérsecute my | soul, and|
take me : yea let him tread my life down upon the
earth, * and láy mine | honour | in the | dust.

---

6 Stand up O Lord in thy wrath, * and lift up thy-    Prayer for
self, because of the indignátion | of mine | enemies :    judgment.
arise up for me in the júdgement | that thou | hast
com-|manded.

7 And so shall the congregation of the péople|
come a-|bout thee : for their sakes thérefore lift | up
thy-|self a-|gain.

8 The Lord shall judge the people ; * give séntence
with | me, O | Lord : according to my righteousness,
and according to the ínnocency | that is | in | me.

9 O let the wickedness of the ungodly come to an
end ; * but guíde | thou the | just : 10 for the righteous
God * tríeth the | very | hearts and | reins.

---

11 My hélp | cometh · of | God : who preserveth    God re-
thém | that are | true of | heart.    quites
certainly
12 God is a righteous Júdge, | strong, and | patient :    if slowly
and Gód is pro-|voked | every | day.

13 If a man will not túrn, he will | whet his | sword :
he hath bént his | bow, and | made it | ready.

14 He hath prepared for him the ínstru-|ments of|
death : he ordáineth his | arrows · a-|gainst the | per-
secutors.

15 Behold he trávail-|eth with | mischief : he hath
conceived sórrow and | brought | forth un-|godliness.

Evil recoils upon the doer.

16 He hath graven and dígged | up a | pit : and is
fallen himself into the destrúction | that he | made for|
other.

17 For his travail shall cóme upon his | own | head :
and his wickedness shall fáll | on his | own | pate.

18 I will give thanks unto the Lord, accórding | to
his | righteousness : and I will praise the Náme | of
the | Lord most | High.

PSALM VIII. *Domine, Dominus noster.*

O | *LORD our* | *Governor* : *how excellent ís thy*|
  *Name in* | *all the* | *world!*

The glory of God through the weak.

Thóu that hast | set thy | glory : a- | — | bove the|
heavens!

2 Out of the mouth of very babes and sucklings
hast thou ordained strength, * becáuse | of thine | ene-
mies : that thou mightest stíll the | enemy, | and·the
a-|venger.

3 For I will consider thy heavens, even the wórks|
of thy | fingers : the moon and the stárs, | which thou|
hast or-|dained.

Man made king

4 What is man, that thóu art | mindful·of | him :
and the són of man, | that thou | visitest | him ?

5 Thou madest him lówer | than the | angels : to
crówn | him with | glory·and | worship.

6 Thou makest him to have dominion of the wórks|
of thy | hands : and thou hast put all things ín sub-|
jection | under·his | feet ;

over the world.

7 All | sheep and | oxen : yéa, and the | beasts|
of the | field ;

8 The fowls of the air, and the físhes | of the | sea :
and whatsoever wálketh through the | paths | of the|
seas.

9 Ó | Lord our | Governor : how excellent is thy|    The glory
Name in | all the | world !    of God.

### Morning Prayer.
### PSALM IX. Confitebor tibi.

I WILL give thanks unto thee O Lórd with my|    Thanks-
whole | heart : I will spéak of | all thy | marvel-   giving to
   God.
lous | works.

2 I will be glád and re-|joice in | thee : yea my
songs will I máke of thy | Name, O | thou most|
Highest.

3 While mine énemies are | driven | back : they    The righ-
   teous
shall fáll and | perish | at thy | presence.    Judge.

4 For thou hast maintained my right | and my|
cause : thou art sét in the | throne that | judgest|
right.

5 Thou hast rebuked the heathen, and destróyed|
the un-|godly : thou hast put oút their | name for|
ever·and | ever.

6 O thou enemy, destructions are cóme to a per-|
petual | end : even as the cities which thou hast de-
stroyed ; * théir me-|morial is | perished | with them.

7 But the Lórd shall en-|dure for | ever : he hath
álso pre-|pared·his | seat for | judgement.

8 For he shall júdge the | world in | righteousness :
and minister trúe | judgement | unto·the | people.

9 The Lord also will be a defénce | for·the op-|
pressed : even a réfuge in | due | time of | trouble.

10 And they that know thy Name will pút their|
trust in | thee : for thou Lord, hast néver | failed|
them that | seek thee.

11 O praise the Lórd which | dwelleth·in | Sion :
shéw the | people | of his | doings.

12 For when he maketh inquisition for blóod he
re-|membereth | them : and forgetteth nót the com-|
plaint | of the | poor.

*Whose praise shall be heard in Sion.*

13 Have mercy upon me O Lord ;\*consider the
trouble which I súffer of | them that | hate me : thou
that liftest me úp | from the | gates of | death.

14 That I may shew all thy praises within the pórts
of the | daughter·of | Sion : Í will re-|joice in | thy
sal-|vation.

15 The heathen are sunk down in the pít | that
they | made : in the same net which they hid prívily|
is their | foot | taken.

*When the heathen are cast down.*

16 The Lord is knówn to | execute | judgement : the
ungodly is trapped in the wórk | of his | own | hands.

17 The wicked shall be túrned | into | hell : and all
the péople | that for-|get | God.

18 For the poor shall not álway | be for-|gotten :
the patient abiding of the méek | shall not | perish·for|
ever.

19 Up Lord, and let not mán have the | upper|
hand : let the heáthen be | judged | in thy | sight.

20 Pút them in | fear, O | Lord : that the heathen
may knów them-|selves to | be but | men.

## PSALM X. *Ut quid, Domine?*

WHY standest thou so fár | off, O | Lord : and hidest thy fáce in the | needful | time of | trouble ?

2 The ungodly for his own lust doth pérse-|cute the | poor : let them be taken in the crafty wíliness| that they | have im-|agined.

3 For the ungodly hath made boast of his ówn | heart's de-|sire : and speaketh good of the cóvet-ous, | whom | God ab-|horreth.  *The oppression of the poor.*

4 The ungodly is so proud that he cáreth| not for | God : néither is | God in | all his| thoughts.

5 His wáys are | alway | grievous : thy judge-ments are far above out of his sight, * and thérefore de-|fieth·he | all his | enemies.

6 For he hath said in his heart, "Tush, I shall néver be | cast | down : there shall nó harm | happen| unto | me."

7 His mouth is full of cúrsing de-|ceit and | fraud : under his tóngue is un-|godli-|ness and | vanity.

8 He sitteth lurking in the thievish córners | of the | streets : and privily in his lurking dens doth he murder the innocent; * his éyes are | set a-|gainst the | poor.

9 For he lieth waiting secretly, * even as a lion lúrketh he | in his | den : thát | he may | ravish·the| poor.

10 Hé doth | ravish · the | poor : whén he | get-teth · him | into his | net.

11 He falleth dówn and | humbleth · him-|self : that the congregation of the poor may fáll into the| hands | of his | captains.

12 He hath said in his heart, "Túsh, | God · hath for-|gotten : he hideth away his fáce, and | he will| never | see it."

13 Arise O Lord God, and líft | up thine | hand : for-|get | not the | poor.    *An appeal to God for help*

14 Wherefore should the wícked blas-|pheme | God : while he doth say in his heart,"Túsh, | thou God | carest · not | for it."

15 Súrely | thou hast | seen it : for thou behóldest un-|godli-|ness and | wrong.

16 That thou mayest táke the matter | into · thine| hand : the poor committeth himself unto thee; * for thóu art the | helper | of the | friendless.

17 Break thou the power of the ungódly | and ma-|licious : take away his ungódliness and | thou shalt | find | none.

18 The Lord is Kíng for | ever · and | ever : and    *which is heard.*
the heáthen are | perished | out · of the | land.

19 Lord, thou hast heard the desíre | of the| poor : thou preparest their heart, and thine éar| hearken-|eth there-|to ;

20 To help the fatherless and póor | unto their| right : that the man of the eárth be no | more ex-| alted · a-|gainst them.

## PSALM XI. *In Domino confido.*

IN the Lórd put | I my | trust : how say ye then    *The coun- sel of fear.*
to my soul that "she should flée as a | bird| unto · the | hill ?"

2 "For lo the ungodly bend their bow, * and make ready their árrows with-|in the | quiver : that

they may privily shoot at thém | which are | true of |
heart."

3 "For the foundátions will be | cast | down : and
whát | hath the | righteous | done?"

4 The Lord is ín his | holy | temple : the Lórd's |
seat | is in | heaven.

5 His éyes con-|sider · the | poor : and his éye-
lids | try the | children · of | men.

6 The Lórd al-|loweth · the | righteous : but the
ungodly, and him that delighteth in wíckedness | doth
his | soul ab-|hor.

7 Upon the ungodly he shall rain snares, fire and
brímstone, | storm and | tempest : thís shall | be their |
portion · to | drink.

8 For the righteous Lórd | loveth | righteousness :
his countenance wíll be-|hold the | thing · that is |
just.

*The
answer of
faith.*

### Ebening Prayer.

### PSALM XII. *Salvum me fac.*

HELP me Lord, for there is not óne | godly ·
man | left : for the faithful are minished fróm
a-|mong the | children · of | men.

2 They talk of vanity évery one | with his | neigh-
bour : they do but flatter with their lips, and dis-
sémble | in their | double | heart.

3 The Lord shall root out áll de-|ceitful | lips :
and the tóngue that | speaketh | proud | things ;

4 Which have said, "With our tóngue will | we
pre-|vail : we are they that ought to speak, whó is |
lord | over | us?"

*The power
and pride
of the
ungodly.*

5 "Now for the comfortless tróubles' sake | of The pro-<br>mise
the | needy : and because of the déep | sighing | of
the | poor,

6 "I will úp," | saith the | Lord : "and will help
every one from him that swelleth agaínst him, | and
will | set him·at | rest."

7 The words of the Lórd are | pure | words : even which<br>cannot<br>fail.
as the silver which from the earth is tried * and
púrified | seven · times | in the | fire.

8 Thou shalt kéep | them, O | Lord : thou shalt
presérve him from | this · gener-|ation · for | ever.

9 The ungodly wálk on | every | side : when they
are exalted, the chíldren of | men are | put · to re-|
buke.


## PSALM XIII. *Usque quo, Domine?*

HOW long wilt thou forgét me O | Lord, for| Complaint.
ever : how lóng wilt thou | hide thy | face
from | me ?

2 How long shall I seek counsel in my soul, *
and be so véxed | in my | heart : how long shall
mine énemies | triumph | over | me ?


3 Consider and héar me O | Lord my | God : Prayer.
lighten mine éyes that I | sleep | not in | death.

4 Lest mine enemy say, Í have pre-|vailed · a-|
gainst him : for if I be cast down, they that tróuble
me | will re-|joice | at it.


5 But my trúst is | in thy | mercy : and my héart Trust.
is | joyful·in | thy sal-|vation.

6 I will sing of the Lord, because he hath déalt
so | lovingly | with me : yea I will praise the Náme |
of the | Lord most | Highest.

## PSALM XIV. *Dixit insipiens.*

THE fool hath saíd | in his | heart : Thére | is |
no | God.

The spirit of folly.

2 They are corrupt and become abóminable | in
their | doings : there is nóne that doeth | good, | no
not | one.

3 The Lord looked down from heaven upón the |
children · of | men : to see if there were any that
would understánd, * and | seek | after | God.

God's sentence.

4 But they are all gone out of the way, they are
altogéther be-|come ab-|ominable : there is nóne that
doeth | good, | no not | one.

5 Their throat is an open sepulchre, with their
tóngues have | they de-|ceived : the póison of | asps
is | under · their | lips.

6 Their mouth is fúll of | cursing · and | bitterness :
their feét are | swift to | shed | blood.

7 Destruction and unhappiness is in their ways,
*and the way of péace have | they not | known : there
is no féar of | God be-|fore their | eyes.

8 "Have they no knowledge, that they are áll
such | workers · of | mischief : eating up my people
as it were bread * and cáll | not up-|on the | Lord?"

9 There were they brought in great fear, éven
where | no fear | was : for God is in the géner-|
ation | of the | righteous.

Its issue.

5

10 As for you, ye have made a mock at the cóunsel | of the | poor : because he pútteth his | trust | in the | Lord.

11 Who shall give salvation unto Ísrael | out of | Sion ? : When the Lord turneth the captívity of his people, * then shall Jacob rejoíce, and | Isra · el | shall be | glad.

### Morning Prayer.

### PSALM XV. *Domine, quis habitabit?*

LORD, who shall dwéll | in thy | tabernacle : or who shall rést up-|on thy | holy | hill ?
2 Even he that léadeth an | uncorrupt | life : and doeth the thing which is right,*and spéaketh the | truth | from his | heart.

*The portraiture of the righteous*

3 He that hath used no deceit in his tongue, * nor done évil | to his | neighbour : ánd | hath not | slandered · his | neighbour.

*in detail.*

4 He that setteth not by himself, but is lówly in his | own | eyes : and maketh múch of | them that | fear the | Lord.

5 He that sweareth unto his neighbour, and dís-ap-|pointeth · him | not : thóugh it | were · to his | own | hindrance.

6 He that hath not given his móney up-|on | usury : nor táken re-|ward a-|gainst the | innocent.

7 Whóso | doeth · these | things : shall | — | never | fall.

## PSALM XVI. *Conserva me, Domine.*

PRESÉRVE | me O | God : for in thée | have
     I | put my | trust. God is man's highest good.

2 O my soul, thou hast sáid | unto · the | Lord :
Thou art my God, my góods are | nothing | unto |
thee.

3 All my delight is upon the sáints that are | in
the | earth : and upon súch | as ex-|cel in | virtue.

4 But they that run after another god shall háve |
great | trouble : 5 Their drink-offerings of blood will
I not offer; * neither make méntion of their | names
with-|in my | lips.

6 The Lord himself is the portion of mine in-
héritance and | of my | cup : thóu | shalt main-|tain
my | lot.

7 The lot is fallen unto mé in a | fair | ground :
yéa, I | have a | goodly | heritage.

8 I will thank the Lórd for | giving · me | warn-
ing : my reins also chásten me | in the | night-|
season. Thankful-ness and trust of the believer.

9 I have set Gód | always · be-|fore me : for he
is on my right hánd, | therefore · I | shall not | fall.

10 Wherefore my heart was glád and my | glory ·
re-|joiced : my flésh | also · shall | rest in | hope.

11 For why? thou shalt not léave my | soul in |
hell : neither shalt thou suffer thy Hóly | One to |
see cor-|ruption.

12 Thou shalt shew me the path of life; * in thy
présence is the | fulness · of | joy : and at thy right
hánd there is | pleasure · for | ever-|more.

## PSALM XVII. *Exaudi, Domine.*

HEAR the right O Lord, considér | my com- | An appeal to God's righteous-ness.
plaint : and hearken unto my prayer, that
góeth not | out of | feigned | lips.

2 Let my sentence come fórth | from thy | pre-sence : and let thine eyes look upón the | thing | that is | equal.

3 Thou hast proved and visited mine heart in the night-season ; * thou hast tried me, and shalt fínd no | wickedness | in me : for I am utterly púrposed that my | mouth shall | not of-|fend.

4 Because of men's works that are done against the wórds | of thy | lips : I have kept me fróm the| ways of | the de-|stroyer.

5 O hold thou up my góings | in thy | paths : thát my | footsteps | slip | not.

6 I have called upon thee O Gód, for | thou shalt| Prayer for protection.
hear me : incline thine éar to me, and | hearken| unto · my | words.

7 Shew thy marvellous loving-kindness, thou that art the Saviour of them which pút their | trust in| thee : from súch as re-|sist | thy right | hand.

8 Keep me as the ápple | of an | eye : hide me únder the | shadow | of thy | wings,

9 From the ungódly that | trouble | me : mine enemies compass me round abóut to | take a-|way my | soul.

10 They are inclósed in their | own | fat : and their móuth | speaketh | proud | things.

11 They lie waiting in our wáy on | every | side : turning their éyes | down | to the | ground ;

12 Like as a lion that is greédy | of his | prey :
and as it were a lion's whélp | lurking·in | secret|
places.

13 Up Lord, disappoínt him and | cast him | down :   Final re-tribution.
deliver my soul from the ungódly which | is a | sword
of | thine ;

14 From the men of thy hand O Lord,*from the
men I say, and fróm the | evil | world : which have
their portion in this life,*whose bellies thou fíllest|
with thy | hid | treasure.

15 They have chíldren at | their de-|sire : and
leave the rést of their | substance | for their | babes.

16 But as for me, I will behóld thy | presence·in|
righteousness : and when I awake up after thy líke-
ness I | shall be | satisfied | with it.


### 𝔈𝔟𝔢𝔫𝔦𝔫𝔤 𝔓𝔯𝔞𝔶𝔢𝔯.

### PSALM XVIII. *Diligam te, Domine.*

I WILL love thee O Lord my strength ;*the Lord   The lesson of the life of faith.
is my stony róck, and | my de-|fence : my Saviour
my God and my might in whom I will trust, * my
buckler, the horn also of mý sal-|vation, | and my|
refuge.

2 I will call upon the Lord, which is wórthy | to
be | praised : só shall I be | safe | from mine |
enemies.

3 The sorrows of déath | compassed | me : and   The be-liever's ex-perience.
the overflowings of ungódliness | made | me a-|
fraid.

4 The pains of héll | came a-|bout me : the snáres
of | death | over-|took me.

5 In my trouble I will cáll up-|on the | Lord : ánd com-|plain | unto my | God.

6 So shall he hear my voice óut of his | holy| temple : and my complaint shall come before him, it shall énter | even | into·his | ears.

7 The éarth | trembled·and | quaked : the very foundations also of the hills shook * and were re-móved be-|cause | he was | wroth.

*The reve-lation of God in His ma-jesty.*

8 There went a smoke oút | in his | presence : and a consuming fire out of his móuth * so that | coals were | kindled | at it.

9 He bowed the heavens álso and | came | down : ánd it was | dark | under·his | feet.

10 He rode upon the chérubims, | and did | fly : he came flying upón the | wings | of the | wind.

11 He made dárkness his | secret | place : his pavilion round about him with dark water, and thick| clouds to | cover | him,

12 At the brightness of his présence his | clouds re-|moved : *háil-|stones, and | coals of | fire.*

13 The Lord also thundered out of heaven, * and the Híghest | gave his | thunder : *háil-|stones, and| coals of | fire.*

14 He sent out his árrows and | scattered | them : he cast forth líghtnings, | and de-|stroyed | them.

15 The springs of waters were seen, * and the foundations of the round world were discóvered at thy | chiding·O | Lord : at the blásting of the | breath of | thy dis-|pleasure.

16 He shall send dówn from on | high to | fetch me : and shall táke me | out of | many | waters.

*Divine help.*

17 He shall deliver me from my strongest enemy,

ánd from | them which | hate me : fór they | are too|
mighty | for me.

18 They prevented me in the dáy | of my | trouble :
bút the | Lord was | my up |holder.

19 He brought me forth also ínto a | place of |
liberty : he brought me forth, even because he hád
a | favour | unto | me.

20 The Lord shall reward me áfter my | righteous|   Man's pre-
dealing : according to the cleanness of my hánds|   paration.
shall he | recompense | me.

21 Because I have kept the wáys | of the | Lord :
and have not forsaken my Gód, | as the | wicked|
doth.

22 For I have an éye unto | all his | laws : and
will not cást out | his com-|mandments | from me.

23 I was also úncor-|rupt be-|fore him : ánd es-|
chewed·mine | own | wickedness.

24 Therefore shall the Lord reward me áfter my|
righteous | dealing : and according unto the cléanness
of my | hands | in his | eye-sight.

25 With the hóly thou | shalt be | holy : and with   The law
a pérfect | man thou | shalt be | perfect.            of God's
                                                      action.
26 With the cléan thou | shalt be | clean : and wíth
the | froward·thou | shalt learn | frowardness.

27 For thou shalt save the péople that are | in ad-|
versity : and shalt bring dówn the | high looks | of
the | proud.

28 Thou álso shalt | light my | candle : the Lord
my God shall máke my | darkness | to be | light.

29 For in thee I shall discómfit an | host of | men :
and with the help of my Gód I shall | leap | over·the|
wall.

30 The way of God is an únde-|filed | way : the
word of the Lord also is tried in the fire ; * he is the
defender of all thém that | put their | trust in|
him.

31 For who is Gód, | but the | Lord : or whó hath
any | strength, ex-|cept our | God ?

32 It is God that gírdeth me with | strength of|
war : ánd | maketh·my | way | perfect.

33 He máketh my | feet like | harts' feet : ánd|
setteth·me | up on | high.

34 He téacheth mine | hands to | fight : and mine
arms shall breák | even·a | bow of | steel.

35 Thou hast given me the defénce of | thy
sal-|vation : thy right hand also shall hold me up,
* and thy lóving cor-|rection·shall | make me|
great.

36 Thou shalt make room enough únder me | for
to | go : thát my | footsteps | shall not | slide.

37 I will follow upon mine énemies and | over-|
take them : neither will I turn agáin till I | have de-|
stroyed | them.

38 I will smite them, that they shall nót be|
able·to | stand : bút | fall | under·my | feet.

39 Thou hast girded me with stréngth | unto·the|
battle : thou shalt throw dówn mine | enemies | under|
me.

40 Thou hast made mine enemies also to túrn
their | backs up-|on me : and Í shall de-|stroy | them
that | hate me.

41 They shall cry, but thére shall be | none to |
help them : yea even unto the Lord shall they crý,|
but he | shall not | hear them.

42 I will beat them as small as the dúst be-|fore the | wind : I will cast them oút as the | clay | in the| streets.

43 Thou shalt deliver me from the strívings | of the | people : and thou shalt máke me the | head | of the | heathen.

44 A péople whom I | have not | known : sháll|—| serve | me.

45 As soon as they héar of me, they | shall o-|bey me : but the stránge children | shall dis-|semble| with me.

46 The stránge | children·shall | fail : ánd be a-| fraid | out of·their | prisons.

47 The Lord liveth, and bléssed be my | strong| helper : and práised be the | God of | my sal-|vation.

48 Even the God that séeth that I | be a-|venged : and subdúeth the | people | unto | me.

49 It is he that delivereth me from my cruel enemies, * and setteth me úp a-|bove mine | adver- saries : thou shalt ríd me | from the | wicked | man.

50 For this cause will I give thanks unto thee O Lórd, a-|mong the | Gentiles : ánd sing | praises| unto·thy | Name.

51 Great prosperity gíveth he | unto·his | King : and sheweth loving-kindness unto David his A- nointed, * and únto his | seed for | ever-|more.

*Thanks- giving in the re- trospect and pros- pect of life.*

## Morning Prayer.

### PSALM XIX. *Caeli enarrant.*

THE heavens decláre the | glory·of | God : and the fírmament | sheweth·his | handy|-work.

*The glory of God in the*

6

2 Óne day | telleth·a-|nother : and óne night | heavens (Nature).
certi-|fieth·an-|other.

3 There is néither | speech nor | language : bút
their | voices·are | heard a-|mong them.

4 Their sound is gone óut into | all | lands : and
their wórds into the | ends | of the | world.

5 In them hath he set a tábernacle | for the | sun :
which cometh forth as a bridegroom out of his
chamber, * and rejoíceth as a | giant·to | run his |
course.

6 It goeth forth from the uttermost part of the
heaven, * and runneth about unto the énd of | it a-|
gain : and there is nothing híd | from the | heat
there-|of.

————————

7 The law of the Lord is an undefiled láw, con-| The glory of God in the Law (Revelation).
verting·the | soul : the testimony of the Lord is súre
and giveth | wisdom | unto·the | simple.

8 The statutes of the Lord are ríght and re-|joice
the | heart : the commandment of the Lord is púre
and giveth | light | unto·the | eyes.

9 The fear of the Lord is cléan and en-|dureth·for|
ever : the judgements of the Lord are trúe, and |
righteous | alto-|gether.

10 More to be desired are they than gold, yéa,
than | much fine | gold : sweeter also than hóney,|
and the | honey-|comb.

11 Moreover by thém is thy | servant | taught : Prayer for guidance.
and in kéeping of them | there is | great re-|ward.

12 Who can téll how | oft he of-|fendeth : O cleanse
thou mé | from my | secret | faults.

13 Keep thy servant also from presumptuous sins,

lest they get the domínion | over | me : so shall I
be undefiled, and ínnocent | from the | great of-|
fence.

14 Let the words of my mouth, and the meditation
of my heart, * be alway accéptable | in thy | sight :
15 O Lord, mý | strength, and | my red-|eemer.


PSALM XX. *Exaudiat te Dominus.*

THE Lord héar thee in the | day of | trouble : The
the Náme of the | God of | Jacob de-|fend people's
thee. prayer.

2 Send thee hélp | from the | sanctuary : ánd |
strengthen · thee | out of | Sion ;

3 Remémber | all thy | offerings : ánd ac-|cept thy|
burnt | sacrifice ;

4 Gránt thee thy | heart's de-|sire : ánd ful-|fil | all
thy | mind.

5 We will rejoice in thy salvation, * and triumph
in the Náme of the | Lord our | God : the Lórd per-|
form all | thy pet-|itions.


6 Now know I that the Lord helpeth his Anointed, * The ruler's
and will héar him from his | holy | heaven : even trust.
with the whólesome | strength of | his right | hand.

7 Some put their trust in cháriots, and | some in|
horses : but we will remember the Náme | of the|
Lord our | God.

8 Théy are brought | down, and | fallen : but wé
are | risen · and | stand | upright.

9 Save Lord and héar us O | King of | heaven :
whén we | call up-|on | thee.

PSALM XXI. *Domine, in virtute tua.*

THE King shall rejóice in thy | strength, O |
Lord : exceeding glád shall he | be of | thy
sal-|vation.

2 Thou hast gíven him his | heart's de-|sire : and
hast not denfed him the re-|quest | of his | lips.

3 For thou shalt prevént him with the | bless-
ings·of | goodness : and shalt set a crówn of pure|
gold up-|on his | head.

4 He asked life of thee, and thou gávest him a|
long | life : éven for | ever | and | ever.

5 His honour is gréat in | thy sal-|vation : glory
and great wórship | shalt thou | lay up-|on him.

6 For thou shalt give him éver-|lasting·fe-|licity :
and make him glád with the | joy | of thy | coun-
tenance.

7 And why? because the King putteth his trúst |
in the | Lord : and in the mercy of the most Híghest |
he shall | not mis-|carry.

8 All thine énemies shall | feel thy | hand : thy
right hánd shall | find out | them that | hate thee,

9 Thou shalt make them like a fiery oven in tíme|
of thy | wrath : the Lord shall destroy them in his
displeasure,*ánd the | fire | shall con-|sume them.

10 Their fruit shalt thou root óut | of the | earth :
and their séed from a-|mong the | children · of|
men.

11 For they intended míschief a-|gainst | thee : and
imagined such a device as they áre not | able | to
per-|form.

12 Therefore shalt thou pút | them to | flight : and

The pros-
perity of
the King.

Ilis future
success.

the strings of thy bow shalt thou make réady a-|gainst the | face of | them.

13 Be thou exalted Lórd in thine | own | strength : só will we | sing, and | praise thy | power.

### Œbening Prayer.

## PSALM XXII. *Deus, Deus meus.*

M Y God my God look upon me; whý hast thou for-|saken | me : and art so far from my health, and fróm the | words of | my com-|plaint ?

*The cry of the for-saken.*

2 O my God I cry in the day-time, bút thou | hear-est | not : and in the níght-season | also·I | take no| rest.

3 And thóu con-|tinuest | holy : Ó thou | wor-ship·of | Isra-|el.

4 Our fáthers | hoped·in | thee : they trusted in thee, and thóu | didst de-|liver | them.

5 They cálled upon thee | and were | holpen : they put their trúst in thee | and were | not con-|founded.

6 But as for me, I am a wórm, and | no | man : a very scorn of mén and the | outcast | of the | people.

7 All they that see me láugh | me to | scorn : they shoot out their líps, and | shake their | heads, | saying,

8 He trusted in God, that hé would de-|liver | him : lét him de-|liver · him, | if he · will | have him.

9 But thou art he that took me oút of my | mo-ther's | womb : thou wast my hope, when I hanged yét up-|on my | mother's | breasts.

*Affliction issuing in prayer.*

10 I have been left unto thee ever sínce | I was| born : thou art my Gód even | from my | mother's| womb.

11 O go not from me, for tróuble is | hard at|
hand : ánd | there is | none to | help me.

12 Many óxen are | come a-|bout me : fat bulls of
Basan clóse me | in on | every | side.

13 They gápe upon me | with their | mouths : as
it were a rámping | and a | roaring | lion.

14 I am poured out like water, * and all my bónes
are | out of | joint : my heart also in the midst of my
bódy is | even·like | melting | wax.

15 My strength is dried up like a potsherd, * and
my tongue cléaveth | to my | gums : and thou shalt
bríng me | into·the | dust of | death.

16 For many dógs are | come a-|bout me : and the
council of the wícked | layeth | siege a-|gainst me.

17 They pierced my hands and my feet; * I may
téll | all my | bones : they stánd | staring·and | look-
ing·up-|on me.

18 They párt my | garments·a-|mong them : and
cást | lots up-|on my | vesture.

19 But be not thou fár from | me, O | Lord : thou
art my súccour, | haste | thee to | help me.

20 Deliver my sóul | from the | sword : my dárling
from the | power | of the | dog.

21 Sáve me from the | lion's | mouth : thou hast
heard me also from amóng the | horns | of the | uni-
corns.

----

22 I will declare thy Náme | unto·my | brethren : Praise of
in the midst of the cóngreg-|ation | will I | praise  God for
thee.                                                His mercy.

23 O praise the Lórd, | ye that | fear him : mag-
nify him all ye of the seed of Jacob, * and fear him áll
ye | seed of | Isra-|el ;

24 For he hath not despised nor abhorred the low estáte | of the | poor : he hath not hid his face from him, * but when he cálled | unto | him he | heard him.

25 My praise is of thee in the gréat | congreg-|a-tion : my vows will I perfórm in the | sight of | them that | fear him.

26 The poor shall éat, | and be | satisfied : they that seek after the Lord shall praíse him ; * your| heart shall | live for | ever.

27 All the ends of the world shall remember them-selves, and be túrned | unto·the | Lord : and all the kíndreds of the | nations·shall | worship·be-|fore him. Acknow-ledgment of His sovereign-ty.

28 For the kíngdom | is the | Lord's : and he is the Góvern-|or a-|mong the | people.

29 All súch as be | fat up-·on | earth : háve| eaten, | and | worshipped.

30 All they that go down into the dúst shall | kneel be-|fore him : and nó man hath | quickened·his | own| soul.

31 Mý | seed shall | serve him : they shall be counted unto the Lórd | for a | gener-|ation.

32 They shall come, and the héavens shall de-| clare his | righteousness : unto a people that shall be bórn, | whom the | Lord hath | made.

## PSALM XXIII. *Dominus regit me.*

THE Lórd | is my | shepherd : thérefore | can I | lack | nothing. The Lord the true Shepherd,

2 He shall féed me in a | green | pasture : and lead me fórth be-|side the | waters·of | comfort.

3 Hé shall con-|vert my | soul : and bring me Guide and
forth in the paths of ríghteousness | for his | Name's|
sake.

4 Yea though I walk through the valley of the
shadow of déath I will | fear no | evil : for thou art
with me; * thy ród and thy | staff | comfort | me.

5 Thou shalt prepare a table before me against Sustainer.
thém that | trouble | me : thou hast anointed my head
with oíl * and my | cup | shall be | full.

6 But thy loving-kindness and mercy shall follow
me all the dáys | of my | life : and I will dwell in the
hóuse | of the | Lord for | ever.

## 𝔐orning 𝔓rayer.

## PSALM XXIV. *Domini est terra.*

THE earth is the Lord's, and áll that | therein| The Sove-
    is : the compass of the wórld, and | they that| reignty of
dwell there-|in.                                the Lord.

2 For he hath fóunded it up-|on the | seas : and
prepáred | it up-|on the | floods.

3 Who shall ascend into the híll | of the | Lord : or His true
who shall rise úp | in his | holy | place?           worship-
                                                     pers.

4 "Even he that hath clean hánds and a | pure|
heart : and that hath not lift up his mind unto vanity,*
nór | sworn to·de-|ceive his | neighbour.

5 "He shall receive the bléssing | from the | Lord :
and righteousness fróm the | God of | his sal-|vation.

6 "This is the generátion of | them that | seek
him : even of thém that | seek thy | face, O | Jacob."

7  "*Lift up your heads O ye gates,* * *and be ye lift up ye éver-|lasting | doors : and the King of | glory| shall come | in.*"

IIis welcome to His sanctuary.

8 "Whó is the | King of | glory?" :

"It is the Lord strong and mighty, * éven the| Lord | mighty·in | battle."

9 "*Lift up your heads O ye gates,* * *and be ye lift up ye éver-|lasting | doors : and the King of | glory| shall come | in.*"

10 "Whó is the | King of | glory?" :

"Even the Lord of hósts, * | he·is the | King of| glory."


## PSALM XXV. *Ad te, Domine, levavi.*

UNTO thee O Lord will I lift up my soul ; * my God I have pút my | trust in | thee : O let me not be confounded, * neither let mine énemies| triumph | over | me.

Confidence.

2  For all they that hope in thée shall | not·be a-|shamed : but such as transgress without a cáuse| shall be | put·to con-|fusion.

3 Shéw me thy | ways, O | Lord : ánd | teach | me thy | paths.

Prayer for personal guidance and forgiveness.

4 Lead me fórth in thy | truth, and | learn me : for thou art the God of my salvation ; * in thée hath been my | hope | all the·day | long.

5 Call to remembrance O Lórd, thy | tender | mercies : and thy loving-kindnesses, whích | have been| ever·of | old.

6 O remember not the sins and offénces | of my|

youth : but according to thy mercy think thou upon mé, * O | Lord, | for thy | goodness.

7 Gracious and ríghteous | is the | Lord : therefore will he téach | sinners | in the | way.

8 Them that are méek shall he | guide in | judgement : and such as are géntle, | them·shall he | learn his | way.

9 All the paths of the Lórd are | mercy·and| truth : unto such as kéep his | covenant, | and his| testimonies.

10 For thy Náme's | sake, O | Lord : be merciful únto my | sin, for | it is | great.

11 What man is hé, that | feareth·the | Lord : him shall he téach in the | way that | he shall | choose.

12 His sóul shall | dwell at | ease : and his séed| shall in-|herit·the | land.

13 The secret of the Lord is amóng | them that| fear him : and hé will | shew |˙them his | covenant.

14 Mine eyes are ever lóoking | unto·the | Lord : for he shall plúck my | feet | out of·the | net.

15 Turn thee unto mé and have | mercy·up-|on me : fór I am | desolate, | and in | misery. *Prayer for forgiveness.*

16 The sorrows of my héart | are en-|larged : O bríng thou | me | out of·my | troubles.

17 Look upon my advérsi-|ty and | misery : ánd for-|give me | all my | sin.

18 Consider mine énemies how | many·they | are : and they béar a | tyrannous | hate a-|gainst me.

19 O keep my sóul, | and de-|liver me : let me not be confounded, fór I have | put my | trust in | thee.

20 Let perfectness and righteous déaling | wait up-|on me : fór my | hope hath | been in | thee.

21 Deliver Ísra-|el, O | God : oút | — of | all his|
troubles.


PSALM XXVI. *Judica me, Domine.*

BE thou my Judge O Lord, for Í have | walked|
innocently : my trust hath been also in the Lórd,|
therefore | shall I·not | fall.

The
pleadings
of a right-
eous soul.

2 Exámine me O | Lord, and | prove me : try óut
my | reins | and my | heart.

3 For thy loving-kindness is éver be-|fore mine|
eyes : and Í will | walk | in thy | truth.

4 I have not dwélt with | vain | persons : neither
will Í have | fellowship | with·the de-|ceitful.

5 I have hated the congregátion | of the | wicked :
and wíll not | sit a-|mong·the un-|godly.

6 I will wash mine hands in ínnocency | O | Lord :
ánd | so will I | go·to thine | altar;

7 That I may shew the vóice of | thanks-|giving :
and téll of | all thy | wondrous | works.

8 Lord, I have loved the habitátion | of thy | house :
and the pláce | where thine | honour | dwelleth.

9 O shut not up my sóul | with the | sinners : nor
my life | with the | blood-|thirsty;

10 Ín whose | hands is | wickedness : ánd their
right | hand is | full of | gifts.

11 But as for mé, I will | walk | innocently : O
deliver me, ánd be | merciful | unto | me.

12 My fóot | standeth | right : I will praise the
Lórd | in the | congreg-|ations.

## PSALM XXVII. *Dominus illuminatio.*

THE Lord is my light and my salvation ; whóm
then | shall I | fear : the Lord is the strength of
my life ; of whóm then | shall I | be a-|fraid ?

Confidence.

2 When the wicked, even mine enemies and my
foes, came upon me to éat | up my | flesh : théy|
stumbled | and | fell.

3 Though an host of men were laid against me, yet
shall not my héart | be a-|fraid : and though there
rose up war against me, yét will I | put my | trust in|
him.

4 One thing have I desired of the Lórd, which
I | will re-|quire : even that I may dwell in the house
of the Lord all the days of my life ; * to behold the fair
beauty of the Lórd, | and to | visit his | temple.

5 For in the time of trouble he shall híde me | in
his | tabernacle : yea in the secret place of his dwelling shall he hide me, * and set me úp up-|on a | rock
of | stone.

6 And now shall he líft | up mine | head : abóve
mine | enemies | round a-|bout me.

7 Therefore will I offer in his dwelling an oblátion
with | great | gladness : I will síng, and speak|
praises | unto the | Lord.

8 Hearken unto my voice O Lord, when I crý|
unto | thee : have mércy up-|on | me, and | hear me.

Prayer.

9 My heart hath talked of thee, Séek | ye my | face :
Thy fáce, | Lord, | will I | seek.

10 O hide not thóu thy | face from | me : nor cast
thy sérvant a-|way | in dis-|pleasure.

11 Thóu hast | been my | succour : leave me not neither forsáke me, O | God of | my sal-|vation.

12 When my fáther and my | mother · for-|sake me : the | Lord | taketh me | up.

13 Téach me thy | way, O | Lord : and lead me in the right wáy, be-|cause | of mine | enemies.

14 Deliver me not over into the wíll | of mine| adversaries : for there are false witnesses risen up agáinst me, and | such as | speak | wrong.

15 I should útter-|ly have | fainted : but that I believe verily to see the goodness of the Lórd in the | land | of the | living. *Renewed confi-dence.*

16 O tárry thou the | Lord's | leisure : be strong and he shall comfort thine heart; * and pút thou thy| trust | in the | Lord.


## PSALM XXVIII. *Ad te, Domine.*

UNTO thee will I crý, O | Lord my | strength : think no scorn of me ; * lest if thou make as though thou hearest not, I become like thém that go| down | into the | pit. *Prayer.*

2 Hear the voice of my humble petitions, when I crý | unto | thee : when I hold up my hands towards the mércy-seat | of thy | holy | temple.

3 O pluck me not away, neither destroy me with the ungódly and | wicked | doers : which speak friendly to their neighbours, * but imágine | mischief | in their| hearts.

4 Reward them accórding | to their | deeds : and according to the wíckedness | of their | own in-| ventions.

5 Recompense them after the wórk | of their| hands : páy them | that they | have de-|served.

6 For they regard not in their mind the works of the Lord, * nor the operátion | of his | hands : therefore shall he break them dówn, | and not | build them | up.

7 Práised | be the | Lord : for he hath heard the vóice | of my | humble pet-|itions.

8 The Lord is my strength and my shield; * my heart hath trusted in hím, and | I am | helped : therefore my heart danceth for joy;*and ín my | song | will I | praise him.

9 The Lórd | is my | strength : and he is the whólesome de-|fence of | his An-|ointed.

10 O save thy people, * and give thy bléssing unto| thine in-|heritance : féed them and | set them | up for | ever.

*Thanksgiving for prayer answered.*

## PSALM XXIX. *Afferte Domino.*

BRING unto the Lord O ye mighty, bring young ráms | unto the | Lord : ascríbe unto the | Lord| worship and | strength.

2 Give the Lord the honour dúe | unto his | Name : wórship the | Lord with | holy | worship.

*Praise the Lord.*

3 It is the Lórd that com-|mandeth the | waters : it is the glórious | God, that | maketh the | thunder.

4 It is the Lord that ruleth the sea, * the voice of the Lord is míghty in | oper-|ation : the vóice of the |Lord·is a | glorious | voice.

5 The voice of the Lórd | breaketh the | cedar-

*The majesty of the Lord in the storm.*

trees : yea the Lórd | breaketh the | cedars of |
Libanus.

6 He maketh them also to skíp | like a | calf :
Libanus also and Sírion, | like a | young | unicorn.

7 The voice of the Lord divideth the flames of
fire ;*the voice of the Lórd | shaketh the | wilderness :
yea the Lord sháketh the | wilder-|ness of | Cades.

8 The voice of the Lord maketh the hinds to bring
forth young, * and discóvereth the | thick | bushes :
in his témple doth | every man | speak of · his | honour.

9 The Lord sítteth a-|bove the | water-flood : and The Lord
the Lórd re-|maineth a | King for | ever.          is King.

10 The Lord shall give stréngth | unto his | people :
the Lord shall give his | people the | blessing of |
peace.

### 𝔐orning 𝔓rayer.

PSALM XXX. *Exaltabo te, Domine.*

I WILL magnify thee O Lord, for thóu hast | set Thanks-
me | up : and not made my fóes to | triumph| giving.
over | me.

2 O Lord my God, I críed | unto | thee : ánd|
thou hast | healed | me.

3 Thou Lord hast brought my sóul | out of | hell :
thou hast kept my life from thém that go | down | to
the | pit.

4 Sing praises unto the Lórd, O ye | saints of | his : Ground of
and give thanks unto him fór a re-|membrance | of praise.
his | holiness.

5 For his wrath endureth but the twinkling of an eye, ánd in his | pleasure is | life : heaviness may endure for a night, * but jóy | cometh | in the | morning.

6 And in my prosperity I said, I shall néver | be re-|moved : thou Lord of thy góodness hast | made my | hill so | strong.    Changes of life.

7 Thou didst túrn thy | face from | me : ánd | I| was | troubled.

8 Then cried I únto | thee, O | Lord : and gát me | to my | Lord right | humbly.

9 "What profit ís there | in my | blood : whén I go | down | to the | pit ?

10 "Shall the dust give thánks | unto | thee : ór shall | it de-|clare thy | truth ?

11 "Hear O Lórd, and have | mercy up-|on me : Lórd, be | thou | my | helper."

12 Thou hast turned my héaviness | into | joy : thou hast put off my sáckcloth and | girded | me with| gladness.    Deliverance.

13 Therefore shall every good man sing of thy práise with-|out | ceasing : O my God, I will give thánks | unto | thee for | ever.

## PSALM XXXI. *In te, Domine, speravi.*

IN thee O Lórd, have I | put my | trust : let me never be put to confúsion, * de-|liver me | in thy| righteousness.    Prayer in trust.

2 Bow dówn thine | ear to | me : máke | haste · to de-|liver | me.

3 And be thou my strong rock, and hóuse | of de-| fence : thát | thou mayest | save | me.

4 For thou art my strong róck, | and my | castle :
be thou also my guide, and léad me | for thy | Name's |
sake.

5 Draw me out of the net that they have láid | pri-
vily | for me : fór | thou | art my | strength.

6 Into thy hánds I com-|mend my | spirit : for thou
hast redéemed me O | Lord, thou | God of | truth.

7 I have hated them that hóld of super-|stitious |
vanities : and my trúst hath | been | in the | Lord.

8 I will be glad and rejoíce | in thy | mercy : for
thou hast considered my trouble, * and hast knówn
my | soul | in ad-|versities.

9 Thou hast not shut me up into the hánd | of the |
enemy : but hast set my féet | in a | large | room.

10 Have mercy upon me O Lórd, for I | am in | Picture
trouble : and mine eye is consumed for very heavi- of distress.
ness; yéa, my | soul | and my | body.

11 For my life is wáxen | old with | heaviness : ánd
my | years | with | mourning.

12 My strength faileth me, becáuse of | mine in-|
iquity : ánd my | bones | are con-|sumed.

13 I became a reproof among all mine enemies, but
espécially a-|mong my | neighbours : and they of mine
acquaintance were afraid of me ; * and they that did
see me withóut con-|veyed them-|selves | from me.

14 I am clean forgotten, as a déad man | out of |
mind : I am becóme | like a | broken | vessel.

15 For I have heard the blásphemy | of the | mul-
titude : and fear is on every side, * while they conspire
together against me, * and take their cóunsel to | take
a-|way my | life.

16 But my hope hath béen in | thee, O | Lord : I Confession and prayer.
have sáid, | " Thou | art my | God."

17 My time is in thy hand; deliver me from the
hánd | of mine | enemies : ánd from | them that | per-
secute | me.

18 Shew thy servant the líght | of thy | counte-
nance : and sáve me | for thy | mercy's | sake.

19 Let me not be confounded O Lord, for Í have |
called up-|on thee : let the ungodly be put to con-
fusion, and be pút to | silence | in the | grave.

20 Let the lying líps be | put to | silence : which
cruelly disdainfully and despítefully | speak a-|gainst
the | righteous.

21 O how plentiful is thy goodness, which thou Thanks-giving.
hast laid úp for | them that | fear thee : and that thou
hast prepared for them that put their trust in thee,
éven be-|fore the | sons of | men!

22 Thou shalt hide them privily by thine own pre-
sence fróm the pro-|voking of | all men : thou shalt
keep them secretly in thy tábernacle | from the | strife
of | tongues.

23 Thánks be | to the | Lord : for he hath shewed
me marvellous great kíndness | in a | strong | city.

24 And whén I made | haste, I | said : " I am cast
oút of the | sight | of thine | eyes."

25 Nevertheless, thou heardest the vóice | of my |
prayer : whén I | cried | unto | thee.

26 O love the Lórd, all | ye his | saints : for the The Lord recom-penseth.
Lord preserveth them that are faithful, * and plénte-
ously re-|wardeth the | proud | doer.

27 Be strong, and hé shall e-|stablish your | heart :
all ye that pút your | trust | in the | Lord.

*Evening Prayer.*

## PSALM XXXII. *Beati, quorum.*

BLESSED is he whose unríghteousness | is for-|
given : ánd whose | sin | is | covered. The bless-<br>edness and<br>condition<br>of forgive-<br>ness.

2 Blessed is the man unto whom the Lórd im-|
puteth no | sin : ánd in whose | spirit thcre | is no |
guile.

3 For whíle I | held my | tongue : my bones con-
sumed awáy | through my | daily com-|plaining.

4 For thy hand is heávy upon me | day and | night :
and my moísture is | like the | drought in | summer.

5 I will acknowledge my sín | unto | thee : and
mine unríghteousness | have I | not | hid.

6 I said I will confess my síns | unto the | Lord :
and so thou forgávest the | wickedness | of my | sin.

7 For this shall every one that is godly make his Rest in<br>the Lord.
prayer unto thee, in a tíme when thou | mayest be |
found : but in the great water-floods * théy shall |
not come | nigh | him.

8 Thou art a place to hide me in, thou shalt pre-
sérve | me from | trouble : thou shalt compass me
abóut with | songs | of de-|liverance.

9 I will inform thee and teach thee in the wáy
wherein | thou shalt | go : and Í will | guide thee |
with mine | eye.

10 Be ye not like to horse and mule, which háve no|
under-|standing : whose mouths must be held with bit
and brídle, * | lest they | fall up-|on thee.

11 Great plagues remaín for | the un-|godly : but

8 --2

whoso putteth his trust in the Lord, mercy embráceth | him on | every | side.

12 Be glad O ye righteous, and rejoíce | in the | Lord : and be jóyful, all | ye · that are | true of | heart.

## PSALM XXXIII. *Exultate, justi.*

REJOICE in the Lórd, | O ye | righteous : for it becometh wéll the | just | to be | thankful.

2 Praíse the | Lord with | harp : sing praises unto him with the lúte, and | instrument | of ten | strings.

3 Sing unto the Lórd a | new | song : sing praises lustily unto hím | with a | good | courage.

4 For the wórd of the | Lord is | true : ánd | all his | works are | faithful.

5 He loveth ríghteous-|ness and | judgement : the earth is fúll of the | goodness | of the | Lord.

6 By the word of the Lórd were the | heavens | made : and all the hosts of them bý the | breath | of his | mouth.

7 He gathereth the waters of the sea together, as it wére up-|on an | heap : and layeth up the déep, as | in a | treasure | house.

8 Let all the eárth | fear the | Lord : stand in awe of him, áll ye that | dwell | in the | world.

9 For he spáke, and | it was | done : he commánded, | and it | stood | fast.

10 The Lord bringeth the cóunsel of the | heathen to | nought : and maketh the devices of the people to be of none effect, and cásteth | out the | counsels of | princes.

*Marginal notes:*
Praise the Lord.

His truth and righteousness.

His creative power.

His government of men.

11 The counsel of the Lórd shall en-|dure for | ever : and the thoughts of his heart from géner-|ation to | gener-|ation.

12 Blessed are the people whose Gód is the | Lord Je-|hovah : and blessed are the folk that he hath chosen to hím to | be | his in-|heritance.

13 The Lord looked down from heaven, and be-héld all the | children of | men : from the habitation of his dwelling he considereth áll them that | dwell | on the | earth.

14 He fashioneth áll the | hearts of | them : and únder-|standeth | all their | works.

15 There is no king that can be saved by the múltitude | of an | host : neither is any mighty mán de-|livered by | much | strength.

16 A horse is counted but a vaín thing to | save a | man : neither shall he deliver ány man | by his | great | strength.

17 Behold the eye of the Lord is upón | them that | fear him : and upon them that pút their | trust | in his | mercy ;

18 To delíver their | soul from | death : and to féed them | in the | time of | dearth.

19 Our soul hath patiently tárried | for the | Lord : for hé is our | help, | and our | shield.

*Confidence in Him.*

20 For our heárt shall re-|joice in | him : because we have hóped | in his | holy | Name.

21 Let thy merciful kindness O Lórd, | be upon | us : like as wé do | put our | trust in | thee.

PSALM XXXIV. *Benedicam Domino.*

I WILL alway give thánks | unto the | Lord : his Praise
praíse shall | ever be | in my | mouth.                    the Lord.

2 My soul shall make her bóast | in the | Lord : the
humble shall héar there-|of, | and be | glad.

3 O praíse the | Lord with | me : and let us mág-
ni-|fy his | Name to-|gether.

4 I sought the Lórd, | and he | heard me : yea he   He is a
delívered me | out of | all my | fear.                     sure Help.

5 They had an eye unto hím, | and were | light-
ened : ánd their | faces were | not a-|shamed.

6 Lo the poor crieth, and the Lórd | heareth | him :
yea and sáveth him | out of | all his | troubles.

7 The angel of the Lord tarrieth róund about |
them that | fear him : ánd | — de-|livereth | them.

8 O taste and see how grácious the | Lord | is :  Make trial
bléssed is the | man that | trusteth in | him.           of His
                                                          Grace.
9 O fear the Lord, yé that | are his | saints : for
théy that | fear him | lack | nothing.

10 The lions do láck, and | suffer | hunger : but
they who seek the Lord shall want no mánner of |
thing | that is | good.

11 Come ye children and héarken | unto | me : I
will téach you the | fear | of the | Lord.

12 What man is hé that | lusteth to | live : ánd
would | fain | see good | days ?

13 Kéep thy | tongue from | evil : and thy líps, |
that they | speak no | guile.

14 Eschew évil, and | do | good : séek | peace, |
and en-|sue it.

15 The eyes of the Lórd are | over the | righteous : *He will deliver and judge.*
and his éars are | open | unto their | prayers.

16 The countenance of the Lord is against thém
that | do | evil : to root out the remémbrance | of
them | from the | earth.

17 The righteous cry, and the Lórd | heareth |
them : and delívereth them | out of | all their |
troubles.

18 The Lord is nigh unto them that áre of a |
contrite | heart : and will save súch as be | of an |
humble | spirit.

19 Great are the troúbles | of the | righteous : but
the Lord delívereth | him | out of | all.

20 He kéepeth | all his | bones : só that not | one
of | them is | broken.

21 But misfortune shall sláy | the un-|godly : and
they that háte the | righteous | shall be | desolate.

22 The Lord delivereth the sóuls | of his | ser-
vants : and all they that put their trúst in | him
shall | not be | destitute.


### Morning Prayer.

## PSALM XXXV. *Judica, Domine.*

PLEAD thou my cause O Lord with thém that | *The Psalmist pleads against his ene-mies.*
strive with | me : and fight thóu against | them
that | fight against | me.

2 Lay hand upón the | shield and | buckler : ánd |
stand | up to | help me.

3 Bring forth the spear, and stop the way against
thém that | persecute | me : say unto my sóul, | I am |
thy sal-|vation.

4 Let them be confounded and put to shame, that séek | after my | soul : let them be turned back and brought to confusion, thát im-|agine | mischief | for me.

5 Let them be as the dúst be-|fore the | wind : and the ángel of the | Lord | scattering | them.

6 Let their wáy be | dark and | slippery : and let the ángel of the | Lord | persecute | them.

7 For they have privily laid their net to destróy me with-|out a | cause : yea even without a cause have they máde a | pit | for my | soul.

8 Let a sudden destruction come upon him una-wares, * and his net that he hath laid prívily | catch him-|self : that he may fáll | into his | own | mis-chief.

9 And my soul, be jóyful | in the | Lord : ít shall re-|joice in | his sal-|vation.

10 All my bones shall say, " Lord who is like unto thee, * who deliverest the poor from hím that is too | strong for | him : yea the poor and him that is in mísery from | him that | spoileth | him ? "

11 False wítnesses did | rise | up : they laid to my cháɾge | things | that I | knew not. *Their cruel ingrati-tude.*

12 They rewárded me | evil for | good : to the gréat dis-|comfort | of my | soul.

13 Nevertheless when they were sick I put on sack-cloth, * and húmbled my | soul with | fasting : and my prayer shall túrn | into mine | own | bosom.

14 I behaved myself as though it had been my fríend, | or my | brother : I went heavily, as óne that | mourneth | for his | mother.

15 But in mine adversity they rejoiced, and gá-

thered them-|selves to-|gether : yea, the very abjects
came together against me unawares, * making móuths
at | me, and | ceased | not.

16 With the flátterers were | busy | mockers : who
gnáshed up-|on me | with their | teeth.

17 Lord how lóng wilt thou | look upon | this : O
deliver my soul from the calamities which they bring
on me, * ánd my | darling | from the | lions.

18 So will I give thee thanks in the gréat | con-
greg-|ation : I will práise | thee a-|mong much |
people.

19 O let not them that are mine enemies triumph
óver | me un-|godly : neither let them wink with
their éyes that | hate me with-|out a | cause.

20 And why? their cómmuning is | not for |
peace : but they imagine deceitful words against thém
that are | quiet | in the | land.

21 They gaped upon me with their | mouths, and |
said : "Fie on thee, fíe on thee we | saw it | with
our | eyes."

22 Thís thou hast | seen, O | Lord : hold not thy
tongue then, * gó not | far from | me, O | Lord.

23 Awake and stand úp to | judge my | quarrel :
avenge thou my cáuse, my | God, | and my | Lord.

24 Judge me O Lord my God accórding | to thy |
righteousness : and lét them not | triumph | over |
me.

25 Let them not say in their hearts, "There, there,
só | would we | have it": neither let them sáy, "We |
have de-|voured | him."

26 Let them be put to confusion and shame to-
gether that rejoíce | at my | trouble : let them be

*Prayer for judgment leading to thanksgiving.*

9

clothed with rebuke and dishónour, that | boast them-|
selves a-|gainst me.

27 Let them be glad and rejoice that fávour my |
righteous | dealing : yea let them say alway, " Blessed
be the Lord * who hath pleasure ín the pro-|sperity |
of his | servant."

28 And as for my tongue, it shall be tálking | of
thy | righteousness : and of thy praíse | all the | day |
long.

## PSALM XXXVI. *Dixit injustus.*

MY heart sheweth me the wíckedness | of · the
un-|godly : that there is nó fear of | God be-|
fore his | eyes.

The reck-
lessness
of the
wicked.

2 For he flattereth himsélf in his | own | sight :
until his abóminable | sin be | found | out.

3 The words of his mouth are unrighteous and fúll |
of de-|ceit : he hath left off to behave himself wísely, |
and to | do | good.

4 He imagineth mischief upon his bed, * and hath
set himsélf in | no good | way : neither doth he ab-
hór | any thing | that is | evil.

5 Thy mercy O Lord réacheth | unto the | heavens :
ánd thy | faithfulness | unto the | clouds.

The un-
failing
goodness
of God.

6 Thy righteousness standeth líke the | strong |
mountains : thy júdgements are | like the | great |
deep.

7 Thou Lord shalt save both man and beast ; *
How excellent ís thy | mercy, O | God : and the
children of men shall put their trust únder the | sha-
dow | of thy | wings.

8 They shall be satisfied with the plénteousness |

of thy | house : and thou shalt give them drink of thy
pléasures as | out | of the | river.

9 For with thée is the | well of | life : and in thy
líght | shall we | see | light.

10 O continue forth thy loving-kíndness unto | them that | know thee : and thy righteoųsness unto thém | that are | true of | heart.    Prayer in confidence.

11 O let not the foot of príde | come a-|gainst me : and ļet not the hánd of the un-|godly | cast me | down.

12 There are they fallen, áll that | work | wicked-ness : they are cast dówn and shall | not be | able to | stand.

## 𝔈𝔟𝔢𝔫𝔦𝔫𝔤 ℜ𝔯𝔞𝔶𝔢𝔯.

## PSALM XXXVII. *Noli aemulari.*

FRET not thyself becáuse of | the un-|godly : nei-ther be thou énvious a-|gainst the | evil | doers.    The just retribution of God.
2 For they shall soon be cut dówn | like the | grass : and be withered éven | as the | green | herb.

3 Put thou thy trust in the Lórd, and be | doing | good : dwell in the land, and vérily | thou | shalt be | fed.    Patience has its reward.

4 Delíght thou | in the | Lord : and he shall gíve | thee thy | heart's de-|sire.

5 Commit thy way unto the Lord, and pút thy | trust in | him : ánd | he shall | bring it to | pass.

6 He shall make thy righteousness as cléar | as the | light : and thy júst | dealing | as the | noon-day.

7 Hold thee still in the Lord, and abide pátiently up-|on | him : but grieve not thyself at him whose

way doth prosper, * against the man that dóeth |
after | evil | counsels.

8 Leave off from wráth and let | go dis-|pleasure :
fret not thyself, élse shalt thou be | moved to | do |
evil.

9 Wicked doers sháll be | rooted | out : and they
that patiently abide the Lórd, | those · shall in-|herit
the | land.

10 Yet a little while, and the ungodly sháll be |
clean | gone : thou shalt look after his pláce, and | he
shall | be a-|way.

11 But the meek-spirited sháll pos-|sess the | earth :
and shall be refréshed in the | multi-|tude of | peace.

12 The ungodly seeketh cóunsel a-|gainst the |
just : and gnásheth up-|on him | with his | teeth.

13 The Lord shall laúgh | him to | scorn : for he
hath séen | that his | day is | coming.

The
strength of
the wicked
is weak-
ness.

14 The ungodly have drawn out the swórd, and
have | bent their | bow : to cast down the poor and
needy, * and to slay such as áre of a | right | conver-|
sation.

15 Their sword shall go thróugh their | own |
heart : ánd their | bow | shall be | broken.

16 A small thing thát the | righteous | hath : is bet-
ter than gréat | riches | of the · un-|godly.

17 For the arms of the ungódly | shall be | broken :
ánd the | Lord up-|holdeth the | rightcous.

18 The Lord knoweth the dáys | of the | godly :
and their inhéritance | shall en-|dure for | ever.

19 They shall not be confóunded in the | perilous |
time : and in the days of déarth | they shall | have
e-|nough.

20 As for the ungodly they shall perish; * and the enemies of the Lord shall consúme as the | fat of | lambs : yea even as the smóke, shall | they con-|sume a-|way.

21 The ungodly borroweth, and páyeth | not a-|gain : but the ríghteous is | merci-|ful, and | liberal.

22 Such as are blessed of Gód shall pos-|sess the | land : and they that are cursed of hím | shall be | rooted | out.

23 The Lord órdereth a | good man's | going : and maketh his wáy ac-|ceptable | to him-|self.

24 Though he fall, he shall nót be | cast a-|way : for the Lórd up-|holdeth him | with his | hand.

25 I have been yóung, and | now am | old : and yet saw I never the righteous forsaken, * nór his | seed | begging their | bread.

26 The righteous is ever mérci-|ful, and | lendeth : ánd his | seed | is | blessed.

27 Flee from evil, and do the thíng | that is | good : ánd | dwell for | ever-|more.

28 For the Lord loveth the thíng | that is | right : he forsaketh not his that be godly, * but théy | are pre-|served for | ever.

29 The unríghteous | shall be | punished : as for the seed of the ungódly, it | shall be | rooted | out.

30 The righteous shall in-|herit the | land : ánd | dwell there-|in for | ever.

The sure reward of the righteous.

31 The mouth of the righteous is éxer-|cised in | wisdom : and his tóngue | will be | talking of | judge-ment.

Counsels of wisdom for life.

32 The law of his Gód is | in his | heart : ánd his | goings | shall not | slide.

33 The ungódly | seeth the | righteous : ánd | seeketh oc-|casion to | slay him.

34 The Lord will not léave him | in his | hand : nór con-|demn him | when he is | judged.

35 Hope thou in the Lord and keep his way, * and he shall promote thee that thóu shalt pos-|sess the | land : when the ungódly shall | perish, | thou shalt | see it.

36 I myself have seen the ungódly in | great | power : and flóurishing | like a | green | bay-tree.

37 I went by, and ló, | he was | gone : I sought him, but his pláce could | no | where be | found.

38 Keep innocency, and take heed unto the thíng | that is | right : for that shall bríng a man | peace | at the | last.

39 As for the transgressors, théy shall | perish to-| gether : and the end of the ungodly is, they shall be róoted | out | at the | last.

40 But the salvation of the righteous cómeth | of the | Lord : who is also their stréngth | in the | time of | trouble.

41 And the Lord shall stánd by | them, and | save them : he shall deliver them from the ungodly and shall save them, * becáuse they | put their | trust in | him.

### 𝔐orning 𝔓rayer.

PSALM XXXVIII. *Domine, ne in furore.*

PUT me not to rebuke O Lórd, | in thine | anger :    <small>Prayer in anguish.</small> neither chásten me | in thy | heavy dis-|pleasure.

2 For thine árrows stick | fast in | me : ánd thy | hand | presseth me | sore.

3 There is no health in my flesh becaúse of | thy Affliction of body.
dis-|pleasure : neither is there any rest in my bónes,
by | reason | of my | sin.

4 For my wickednesses are góne | over my | head :
and are like a sore búrden too | heavy for | me to |
bear.

5   My   wounds   stínk,   and | are   cor-|rupt :
thróugh | — | my | foolishness.

6 I am brought into so gréat | trouble and | misery :
that I go móurning | all the | day | long.

7 For my loins are fílled with a | sore dis-|ease :
and there is no whóle | part | in my | body.

8 I am feéble, and | sore | smitten : I have roared
for the véry dis-|quietness | of my | heart.

9 Lord thou knowest áll | my de-|sire : and my
gróaning | is not | hid from | thee.

10 My heart panteth, my stréngth hath | failed |
me : and the síght of mine | eyes is | gone | from me.

11 My lovers and my neighbours did stand lóoking Afflictions from men.
up-|on my | trouble : and my kínsmen | stood a-|far |
off.

12 They also that sought after my lífe laid | snares
for | me : and they that went about to do me evil
talked of wickedness, * and imagined decéit | all the |
day | long.

13 As for me, I was like a déaf | man, and | heard
not : and as one that is dúmb, who | doth not | open
his | mouth.

14 I became even as a mán that | heareth | not :
ánd in whose | mouth are | no re-|proofs.

15 For in thee O Lórd, have I | put my | trust :     God is the only re- fuge.
thou shalt ánswer for | me, O | Lord my | God.

16 I have required that they, even mine enemies,
should not tríumph | over | me : for when my foot
slipped, théy re-|joiced | greatly a-|gainst me.

17 And I truly am sét | in the | plague : and my
héaviness is | ever | in my | sight.

18 For I wíll con-|fess my | wickedness : ánd be |
sorry | for my | sin.

19 But mine enemies líve, | and are | mighty :
and they that háte me | wrongfully · are | many in |
number.

20 They also that reward evil for góod | are a-|
gainst me : because I fóllow the | thing that |
good | is.

21 Forsake me nót, O | Lord my | God : bé not |
thou | far from | me.

22 Háste thee to | help | me : O Lórd | God of |
my sal-|vation.


## PSALM XXXIX. *Dixi, Custodiam.*

I SAID, I will take héed | to my | ways : that Í     The trial of faith.
of-|fend not | in my | tongue.

2 I will keep my mouth as it wére | with a | bridle :
while the un-|godly is | in my | sight.

3 I held my tóngue, and | spake | nothing : I kept
silence yea even from good words; bút it was | pain
and | grief to | me.

4 My heart was hot within me, * and while I was
thus músing the | fire | kindled : and at the lást I |
spake | with my | tongue ;

5 Lord, let me know mine end, * and the númber | of my | days : that I may be cértified how | long I | have to | live.

6 Behold thou hast made my days as it wére a | span | long : and mine age is even as nothing in respect of thee; * and verily every man líving is | alto-|gether | vanity.

7 For man walketh in a vain shadow, * and disquíeteth him-|self in | vain : he heapeth up riches, and cannot téll | who shall | gather | them.

8 And now Lord, whát | is my | hope : trúly my | hope is | even in | thee.

9 Deliver me from áll | mine of-|fences : and make me nót a re-|buke | unto the | foolish.

10 I became dumb, and ópened | not my | mouth : fór | it was | thy | doing.

11 Take thy plágue a-|way from | me : I am even consumed by the méans | of thy | heavy | hand.

12 When thou with rebukes dost chasten man for sin, * thou makest his beauty to consume away, like as it were a móth | fretting a | garment : évery man | therefore | is but | vanity.

13 Hear my prayer O Lord, * and with thine éars con-|sider my | calling : hóld not thy | peace | at my | tears.

14 For Í am a | stranger with | thee : and a só-journer, as | all my | fathers | were.

15 O spare me a little, that Í may re-|cover my | strength : before I go hénce, and | be no | more | seen.

## PSALM XL. *Expectans expectavi.*

I WAITED pátiently | for the | Lord : and he in-
clíned unto | me, and | heard my | calling.

2 He brought me also out of the horrible pit, óut
of the | mire and | clay : and set my feet upon the
róck, and | ordered | my | goings.

3 And he hath put a new sóng | in my | mouth :
even a thánks-|giving | unto our | God.

4 Mány shall | see it, and | fear : and shall pút
their | trust | in the | Lord.

5 Blessed is the man that hath set his hópe | in
the | Lord : and turned not unto the proud, and to
súch as | go a-|bout with | lies.

6 O Lord my God, great are the wondrous works
which thou hast done, * like as be also thy thóughts
which | are to | us-ward : and yet there is no man that
órdereth | them | unto | thee.

7 If I should decláre them and | speak of | them :
they should be more than Í am | able | to ex-|press.

8 Sacrifice and meat-óffering thou | wouldest | not :
bút mine | ears | hast thou | opened.

9 Burnt-offerings and sacrifice for sín hast thou |
not re-|quired : thén | said I, | Lo, I | come,

10 In the volume of the book it is written of me, *
that I should fulfil thy wíll, | O my | God : I am con-
tent to do it ; * yea thy láw | is with-|in my | heart.

11 I have declared thy righteousness in the gréat |
congreg-|ation : lo I will not refrain my líps, O |
Lord, * and | that thou | knowest.

12 I have not hid thy righteousness with-|in my |
heart : my talk hath been of thy trúth, | and of | thy
sal-|vation.

13 I have not kept back thy lóving | mercy and | truth : fróm the | great | congreg-|ation.

---

14 Withdraw not thou thy mércy from | me, O | Lord : let thy loving-kindness and thy trúth | alway pre-|serve | me.

15 For innumerable troubles are come about me ; * my sins have taken such hold upon me that I am not áble to | look | up : yea they are more in number than the hairs of my head, * ánd my | heart hath | failed | me.

16 O Lord, let it be thy pléasure to de-|liver | me : máke | haste, O | Lord, to | help me.

17 Let them be ashamed and confounded together, * that seek after my sóul | to de-|stroy it : let them be driven backward and pút to re-|buke, * that | wish me | evil.

18 Let them be desolate, ánd re-|warded with | shame : that say unto me, Fíe up-|on thee, | fie up-|on thee.

19 Let all those that seek thee be jóyful and | glad in | thee : and let such as love thy salvation say álway, * The | Lord | be | praised.

20 As for mé I am | poor and | needy : bút the | Lord | careth | for me.

21 Thou art my hélper | and red-|eemer : make nó long | tarrying, | O my | God.

**Ebening Prayer.**

PSALM XLI.  *Beatus qui intelligit.*

B LESSED is he that consídereth the | poor and | needy : the Lord shall delíver him | in the | time of | trouble.

Prayer in distress.

The blessedness of the merciful.

2 The Lord preserve him and keep him alive, *
that he may be bléssed up-|on | earth : and deliver not
thou him ínto the | will | of his | enemies.

3 The Lord comfort him when he lieth síck up-|on
his | bed : make thou áll his | bed | in his | sickness.

4 I said, Lord be mérciful | unto | me : heal my sóul   Desola-
for I have | sinned a-|gainst | thee.   tion.

5 Mine enemies spéak | evil | of me : " When shall
he díe, | and his | name | perish ? "

6 And if he come to sée me, he | speaketh | vanity :
and his heart conceiveth falsehood within himself, *
and when he cómeth | forth he | telleth | it.

7 All mine enemies whisper togéther a-|gainst |
me : even against mé do | they im-|agine this |
evil.

8 " Let the sentence of guíltiness pro-|ceed a-|gainst
him : and now that he lieth, lét him | rise | up no |
more."

9 Yea even mine own familiar fríend, | whom I |
trusted : who did also eat of my bréad, hath [ laid
great | wait for | me.

10 But be thou merciful únto | me, O | Lord : raise   Confi-
thou me up agáin, | and I | shall re-|ward them.   dence in
  present
11 By this I knów thou | favourest | me : that mine   affliction.
énemy | doth not | triumph a-|gainst me.

12 And when I am in my health, thóu up-|holdest |
me : and shalt sét me be-|fore thy | face for | ever.

---

13 *Blessed be the Lord Gód of | Isra-|el : wórld
without | end. | A-|men.*

## PSALM XLII. *Quemadmodum.*

LIKE as the hárt de-|sireth the | waterbrooks : so
longeth my sóul | after | thee, O | God.

An exile recals in sorrow the worship of old time.

2 My soul is athirst for God, yea even fór the | living | God : when shall I come to appéar be-|fore the | presence of | God ?

3 My tears have been my méat | day and | night : while they daily sáy unto me, | " Where is | now thy | God ?"

4 Now when I think thereupon, I pour out my héart | by my-|self : for I went with the multitude, * and brought them fórth | into the | house of | God ;

5 In the voice of práise | and thanks-|giving : amóng | such as | keep | holy-day.

6 *Why art thou so full of héaviness, | O my | soul : and why art thou só dis-|quiet-|ed with-|in me ?*

7 *Pút thy | trust in | God : for I will yet give him thánks for the | help | of his | countenance.*

8 My God, my sóul is | vexed with-|in me : there-fore will I remember thee concerning the land of Jor-dan, * ánd the | little | hill of | Hermon.

His prayer from a strange land.

9 One deep calleth another, because of the nóise of the | water-|pipes : all thy waves and stórms are | gone | over | me.

10 The Lord hath granted his loving-kíndness | in the | daytime : and in the night-season did I sing of him, * and made my prayer únto the | God | of my | life.

11 I will say unto the God of my strength, Why hast thóu for-|gotten | me : why go I thus heavily, while the | enemy op-|presseth | me ?

12 My bones are smitten asúnder | as with a | sword : while mine enemies that tróuble me | cast me | in the | teeth ;

13 Namely while they say dáily | unto | me : " Whére | — is | now thy | God ? "

14 *Why art thou so véxed, | O my | soul : and why art thou só dis-|quiet-|ed with-|in me ?*

15 *O pút thy | trust in | God : for I will yet thank him, which is the help of my | countenance, | and my | God.*

## PSALM XLIII. *Judica me, Deus.*

GIVE sentence with me O God, and defend my cause agáinst the un-|godly | people : O deliver me fróm the de-|ceitful and | wicked | man.

The exile's prayer for restoration to the city and temple of God.

2 For thou art the God of my strength, whý hast thou | put me | from thee : and why go I so heavily, while the | enemy op-|presseth | me ?

3 O send out thy light and thy trúth, that | they may | lead me : and bring me unto thy hóly | hill, and | to thy | dwelling.

4 And that I may go unto the altar of God, * even unto the Gód of my | joy and | gladness : and upon the harp will I give thánks unto | thee, O | God, my | God.

5 *Why art thou so héavy, | O my | soul : and why art thou só dis-|quiet-|ed with-|in me ?*

6 *O pút thy | trust in | God : for I will yet give him thanks, which is the hélp of my | countenance, | and my | God.*

## Morning Prayer.

## PSALM XLIV. *Deus, auribus.*

WE have heard with our ears O Gód, * our | fathers have | told us : what thou hast dóne * | in their | time of | old;

The past mercies of God to Israel.

2 How thou hast driven out the heathen with thy hánd, and | planted them | in : how thou hast destróyed the | nations, and | cast them | out.

3 For they gat not the land in possession thróugh their | own | sword : neither was it their ówn | arm that | helped | them ;

4 But thy right hand and thine arm, and the líght | of thy | countenance : because thou hádst a | favour | unto | them.

5 Thóu art my | King, O | God : sénd | help | unto | Jacob.

The people's trust in Him.

6 Through thee will we óver-|throw our | enemies : and in thy Name will we tread them únder, that | rise | up a-|gainst us.

7 For I will not trúst | in my | bow : it is nót my | sword | that shall | help me ;

8 But it is thou that sávest us | from our | enemies : and púttest them | to con-|fusion that | hate us.

9 We make our boast of Gód | all day | long : ánd will | praise thy | Name for | ever.

10 But now thou art far off, and púttest us | to con-| fusion : and góest not | forth | with our | armies.

Prayer in present national distress.

11 Thou makest us to turn our bácks up-|on our | enemies : so that théy which | hate us | spoil our | goods.

12 Thou lettest us be éaten | up like | sheep : and hast scáttered | us a-|mong the | heathen.

13 Thou séllest thy | people for | nought : ánd | takest no | money | for them.

14 Thou makest us to be rebúked | of our | neigh-bours : to be laughed to scorn, and had in derision of thém | that are | round a-|bout us.

15 Thou makest us to be a bý-word a-|mong the | heathen : and that the péople | shake their | heads at | us.

16 My confúsion is | daily be-|fore me : and the sháme of my | face hath | covered | me ;

17 For the voice of the slánderer | and blas-| phemer : fór the | enemy | and a-|venger.

18 And though all this be come upon us, yét do we | not for-|get thee : nor beháve ourselves | frowardly | in thy | covenant. *Faith unshaken by reverses.*

19 Our héart is not | turned | back : néither our | steps gone | out of thy | way ;

20 No, not when thou hast smitten us ínto the | place of | dragons : and cóvered us | with the | shadow of | death.

21 If we have forgotten the Name of our God,*and holden up our hánds to any | strange | god : shall not God search it out ?*for he knoweth the véry | secrets | of the | heart.

22 For thy sake also are we kílled | all·the day | long : and are counted as shéep ap-|pointed | to be | slain.

23 Up Lord, whý | sleepest | thou : awake, and bé not | absent from | us for | ever. *Call for help.*

24 Wherefore hídest | thou thy | face : and forgét-
test our | miser-|y and | trouble ?

25 For our soul is brought low, éven | unto the |
dust : our bélly | cleaveth | unto the | ground.

26 A-|rise, and | help us : and delíver us | for thy |
mercy's | sake.

## PSALM XLV. *Eructavit cor meum.*

M Y heart is indíting of a | good | matter : I
speak of the things which Í have | made |
unto the | King.

*The beauty of the Divine King.*

2 My tóngue | is the | pen : óf | —a | ready |
writer.

3 Thou art faírer than the | children of | men : full
of grace are thy lips, * because Gód hath | blessed |
thee for | ever.

4 Gird thee with thy sword upon thy thígh, O |
thou most | Mighty : accórding to thy | worship |
and re-|nown.

*His strength in war.*

5 Good lúck have thou | with thine | honour : ride
on, because of the word of truth of meekness and
righteousness; * and thy right hánd shall | teach thee |
terrible | things.

6 Thy arrows are very sharp, * and the people
shall be subdúed | unto | thee : even in the mídst
a-|mong the | King's | enemies.

7 Thy seat O Gód, en-|dureth for | ever : the
sceptre of thy kíngdom | is a | right | sceptre.

*His righteous sovereign-ty.*

8 Thou hast loved ríghteousness and | hated in-|
iquity : wherefore God, even thy God, hath anointed
thee * with the óil of | gladness a-|bove thy | fellows.

9 All thy garments smell of mýrrh, | aloes, and |

*His state.*

11

cassia : out of the ivory palaces, wherebý | they have |
made thee | glad.

10 Kings' daughters were among thy hónour-|able |
women : upon thy right hand did stand the queen
in a vesture of gold, wróught a-|bout with | divers |
colours.

---

11 Hearken O daughter and 'consíder, in-|cline
thine | ear : forget also thine own péople, | and thy |
father's | house.

12 So shall the King have pléasure | in thy |
beauty : for he is thy Lord Gód, and | worship |
thou | him.

13 And the daughter of Tyre shall be thére | with
a | gift : like as the rich also among the people shall
make their súppli-|cation be-|fore | thee.

14 The King's daughter is all glóri-|ous with-|in :
her clóthing | is of | wrought | gold.

15 She shall be brought unto the Kíng in | raiment
of | needle-work : the virgins that be her fellows shall
bear her company, ánd shall be | brought | unto |
thee.

16 With joy and gládness shall | they be |
brought : and shall énter | into the | King's | palace.

17 Instead of thy fáthers thou | shalt have | child-
ren : whom thou mayest máke | princes in | all |
lands.

18 I will remember thy Name from one generá-
tion | to an-|other : therefore shall the people give
thanks unto thée, | world with-|out | end.

*The de-*
*votion and*

*the coming*
*of His*
*Bride.*

*The bless-*
*ing on*
*their*
*union.*

## PSALM XLVI. *Deus noster refugium.*

GÓD is our | hope and | strength : a véry | pre- sent | help in | trouble.

*God is our hope.*

2 Therefore will we not fear, thóugh the | earth be | moved : and though the hills be carried ínto the | midst | of the | sea.

3 Though the waters theréof | rage and | swell : and though the mountains sháke at the | tempest | of the | same.

4 The rivers of the flood thereof shall make glád the | city of | God : the holy place of the tábernacle | of the | most | Highest.

*He will guard and gladden His Holy city,*

5 God is in the midst of her, therefore shall she nót | be re-|moved : Gód shall | help her, and | that right | early.

6 The heathen make much adó and the | kingdoms are | moved : but God hath shewed his voíce, and the | earth shall | melt a-|way.

7 *The Lórd of | hosts is | with us : the Gód of | Jacob | is our | refuge.*

8 O come hither and behold the wórks | of the | Lord : what destruction hé hath | brought up-|on the | earth.

*and es-tablish a kingdom of peace.*

9 He maketh wars to céase in | all the | world : he breaketh the bow and knappeth the spear in sunder, * and búrneth the | chariots | in the | fire.

10 Be still then, and knów that | I am | God : I will be exalted among the heathen, and Í will be ex-|alted | in the | earth.

11 *The Lórd of | hosts is | with us : the Gód of | Jacob | is our | refuge.*

**Ebening Prayer.**

## PSALM XLVII. *Omnes gentes, plaudite.*

O CLAP your hands togéther, | all ye | people : Praise
O sing unto Gód | with the | voice of | melody. God for His con-

2 For the Lord is hígh, and | to be | feared : he is quering Majesty.
the gréat | King upon | all the | earth.

3 He shall subdue the péople | under | us : ánd
the | nations | under our | feet.

4 He shall choose óut an | heritage | for us : even
the wórship of | Jacob, | whom he | loved.

5 God is gone úp with a | merry | noise : and the He has
Lórd with the | sound | of the | trump. triumph-ed.

6 O sing praises, sing praíses | unto our | God : O Praise
sing praíses, sing | praises | unto our | King. God for his uni-
7 For God is the Kíng of | all the | earth : síng versal sovereign
ye | praises with | under-|standing. ty.

8 God reígneth | over the | heathen : God sítteth
up-|on his | holy | seat.

9 The princes of the people are joined unto the
péople of the | God of | Abraham : for God, which is
very high exalted, doth defend the éarth, as it | were |
with a | shield.

## PSALM XLVIII. *Magnus Dominus.*

G REAT is the Lord, and híghly | to be | praised : Sion the
in the city of our God, éven up-|on his | holy | city of God.
hill.

2 The hill of Sion is a fair place, and the jóy of
the | whole | earth : upon the north-side lieth the cíty |
of the | great | King.

God is well knówn | in her | palaces : ás|—a | sure | refuge.

3 For ló the | kíngs of the | earth : are gáthered, *He has protected her;*
and | gone | by to-|gether.

4 They márvelled to | see such | things : they were astónished, and | suddenly | cast | down.

5 Fear came thére upon | them, and | sorrow : ás upon a | woman | in her | travail.

6 Thou shalt break the shíps | of the | sea : through |— the | east | wind.

7 Like as we have heard, so have we seen * in the city of the Lord of hosts, in the cíty | of our | God : Gód up-|holdeth the | same for | ever.

8 We wait for thy lóving-|kindness, O | God : ín *and will protect her.*
the | midst | of thy | temple.

9 O God according to thy Name, * so is thy práise unto the | world's | end : thy ríght | hand is | full of | righteousness.

10 Let the mount Sion rejoice, * and the dáughter of | Judah be | glad : be-|cause | of thy | judgements.

11 Walk about Sion, and gó | round a-|bout her : ánd | tell the | towers there-|of.

12 Mark well her búlwarks, * set | up her | houses : that ye may téll | them that | come | after.

13 For this God is oúr God for | ever and | ever : hé shall be our | guide | unto | death.

### PSALM XLIX.    *Audite haec, omnes.*

O HEAR ye thís, | all ye | people : ponder it with *A great lesson to be learnt.*
your ears, all yé that | dwell | in the | world ;

2 High and lów, | rich and | poor : óne | — | with an-|other.

3 My móuth shall | speak of | wisdom : and my
heárt shall | muse of | under-|standing.

4 I will incline mine eár | to the | parable : and
shéw my dark | speech up-|on the | harp.

5 Wherefore should I féar in the | days of | wick-
edness : and when the wickedness of my heels cóm-
passeth | me | round a-|bout ?

6 There be some that put their trúst | in their |
goods : and boast themsélves in the | multitude | of
their | riches.

7 But no man máy de-|liver his | brother : nor
make agréement | unto | God for | him ;

8 For it cost móre to red-|eem their | souls : so
that he must lét | that a-|lone for | ever;

9 Yéa though he | live | long : ánd | see | not the |
grave.

10 For he seeth that wise men also díe  * and |
perish to-|gether : as well as the ignorant and foólish,
and | leave their | riches for | other.

11 And yet they think that their hóuses shall con-|
tinue for | ever : and that their dwelling-places shall
endure from one generation to another ; * and call the
lánds | after their | own | names.

12 *Nevertheless, man will nót a-|bide in | honour :
seeing he may be compared unto the beasts that perish ;
this | is the | way of | them.*

13 Thís | is their | foolishness : ánd their post-|
erity | praise their | saying.

14 They lie in the hell like sheep, * death gnaweth
upon them, * and the righteous shall have domination
óver them | in the | morning : their beauty shall
consúme in the | sepulchre | out of their | dwelling.

15 But God hath delivered my sóul from the | place
of | hell : fór | he | shall re-|ceive me.

16 Be not thou afraid, thóugh one be | made | rich :
or if the glóry of his | house | be in-|creased ;

17 For he shall carry nothing awáy with him | when
he | dieth : neither sháll his | pomp | follow | him.

18 For while he lived, he counted himsélf an |
happy | man : and so long as thou doest well unto
thyself, mén will | speak | good of | thee.

19 He shall follow the generátion | of his | fathers :
ánd shall | never | see | light.

20 *Man being in honour hath nó | under-|standing :
but is compáred | unto the | beasts that | perish.*

### 𝔐orning 𝔓rayer.

### PSALM L. *Deus deorum.*

THE Lord, even the most míghty | God, hath |    The ap-
spoken : and called the world, * from the rising   pearance
up of the sun, únto the | going | down there-|of.    of God
                                                    for judg-
                                                    ment.

2 Out of Síon hath | God ap-|peared : in |—| per-
fect | beauty.

3 Our God shall cóme, and shall | not keep |
silence : there shall go before him a consuming fire, *
and a mighty tempest sháll be | stirred up | round
a-|bout him.

4 He shall call the héaven | from a-|bove : and the
eárth, that | he may | judge his | people.

5 "Gather my saints togéther | unto | me : those
that have made a cóvenant | with | me with | sa-
crifice."

6 And the héaven shall de-|clare his | righteous-
ness : fór | God is | Judge him-|self.

7 "Hear O my péople and | I will | speak : I my- His sen-
self will testify against thee O Israel; * for I am Gód, | tence on<br>the people
even | thy | God. for false<br>worship.

8 " I will not reprove thee because of thy sacrifices,
ór for thy | burnt-|offerings : becáuse they | were not |
alway be-|fore me.

9 "I will take no búllock | out of thine | house :
nór | he-goat | out of thy | folds.

10 "For all the béasts of the | forest are | mine :
and so are the cáttle up-|on a | thousand | hills.

11 " I know all the fówls up-|on the | mountains :
and the wild béasts of the | field are | in my | sight.

12 " If I be hungry Í | will not | tell thee : for the
whole world is míne, and | all that | is there-|in.

13 " Thinkest thou that Í will | eat bulls' | flesh :
ánd | drink the | blood of | goats ?

14 "Offer unto Gód | thanks-|giving : and pay thy
vóws | unto the | most | Highest.

15 "And call upon mé in the | time of | trouble :
so will I héar thee, and | thou shalt | praise | me."

16 But unto the ungódly | said | God : " Why dost On the un-
thou preach my laws, * and tákest my | covenant | in righteous<br>for break-
thy | mouth ; ing the<br>moral law.

17 "Whereas thou hátest to | be re-|formed : ánd
hast | cast my | words be-|hind thee ?

18 "When thou sawest a thief, thou conséntedst |
unto | him : and hast béen par-|taker | with the ad-|
ulterers.

19 "Thou hast lét thy | mouth speak | wickedness :
and with thy tóngue thou hast | set | forth de-|ceit.

20 "Thou satest, and spákest a-|gainst thy | brother :
yea and hast slándered thine | own | mother's | son.

21 "These things hast thou done, and I held my tongue, * and thou thoughtest wickedly that I am even súch a one | as thy-|self : but I will reprove thee, and set befóre thee the | things that | thou hast | done.

22 "O consider this, yé that for-|get | God : lest I pluck you away, and there be nóne | to de-|liver | you. The sum.

23 "Whoso offereth me thanks and práise, he | honoureth | me : and to him that ordereth his conversation ríght * will I | shew the sal-|vation of | God."

## PSALM LI. *Miserere mei, Deus.*

HAVE mercy upon me O God, áfter thy | great | goodness : according to the multitude of thy mercies dó a-|way | mine of-|fences. Confession and prayer for forgiveness and restoration.

2 Wash me thróughly | from my | wickedness : ánd | cleanse me | from my | sin.

3 Fór I ac-|knowledge my | faults : ánd my | sin is | ever be-|fore me.

4 Against thee only have I sinned, * and done this évil | in thy | sight : that thou mightest be justified in thy sáying, * and | clear when | thou art | judged.

5 Behóld I was | shapen in | wickedness : ánd in| sin hath my | mother con-|ceived me.

6 But lo, thou requirest trúth in the | inward | parts : and shalt make me to únder-|stand | wisdom | secretly.

7 Thou shalt purge me with hýssop and I | shall be | clean : thou shalt wásh me and I | shall be | whiter than | snow.

8 Thou shalt make me héar of | joy and | glad-
ness : that the bones which thóu hast | broken | may
re-|joice.

9 Turn thy fáce | from my | sins : and pút out |
all | my mis-|deeds.

10 Make me a cléan | heart, O | God : and renéw
a | right | spirit with-|in me.

11 Cast me not awáy | from thy | presence : and
táke not thy | holy | Spirit | from me.

12 O give me the cómfort of thy | help a-|gain :
and stáblish me | with thy | free | Spirit.

13 Then shall I teach thy wáys | unto the | wicked :
and sinners sháll be con-|verted | unto | thee.

---

14 Deliver me from blood-guiltiness O God, * thou    *The return
that art the Gód | of my | health : and my tóngue    of thankful
shall | sing | of thy | righteousness.                service.

15 Thou shalt ópen my | lips, O | Lord : ánd my |
mouth shall | shew thy | praise.

16 For thou desirest no sacrifice, élse would I |
give it | thee : but thou delíghtest | not in | burnt-|
offerings.

17 The sacrifice of Gód is a | troubled | spirit : a
broken and contrite heart O Gód, | shalt thou | not
de-|spise.

---

18 O be favourable and grácious | unto | Sion :    *Prayer for
buíld thou the | walls | of Je-|rusalem.              Sion.

19 Then shalt thou be pleased with the sacrifice
of righteousness, with the burnt-ófferings | and ob-|
lations : then shall they óffer young | bullocks up-|on
thine | altar.

## PSALM LII. *Quid gloriaris?*

WHY boastest thou thy·self, thou tyrant, that
thóu canst | do | mischief **:** 2 whereas the
goodness of Gód en-|dureth | yet | daily?

3 Thy tóngue im-|agineth | wickedness **:** and with
lies thou cúttest | like a | sharp | razor.

4 Thou hast loved unrighteousness | more than |
goodness **:** and to tálk of | lies | more than | right-
eousness.

5 Thou hast loved to speak all wórds that | may
do | hurt **:** Ó | thou | false | tongue.

6 Therefore shall God destróy | thee for | ever **:**
he shall take thee and pluck thee out of thy dwelling,
* and root thee oút of the | land | of the | living.

*Rebuke of the wicked.*

*God's judgment.*

7 The righteous also shall sée | this, and | fear **:**
ánd shall | laugh | him to | scorn;

8 "Lo, this is the man * that took not Gód | for
his | strength **:** but trusted unto the multitude of his
riches, * and stréngthened him-|self | in his | wick-
edness."

9 As for me, I am like a green ólive-tree in the |
house of | God **:** my trust is in the tender mércy of |
God for | ever and | ever.

10 I will always give thanks unto thee for thát |
thou hast | done **:** and I will hope in thy Náme for
thy | saints | like it | well.

*The awe and the trust of the righteous.*

### Ebening Prayer.

## PSALM LIII. *Dixit insipiens.* (Compare Ps. xiv.)

THE foolish body hath sáid | in his | heart **:**
Thére | is | no | God.

*The spirit of folly.*

12—2

2 Corrupt are they, and become abóminable | in their | wickedness : thére is | none that | doeth | good.

3 God looked down from heaven upón the | children of | men : to see if there were any, that would under-stánd, * and | seek | after | God.

God's sen-tence.

4 But they are all gone out of the way, they are altogéther be-|come ab-|ominable : there is also none that dóeth | good, | no not | one.   ˙

5 "Are not they without understánding that | work | wickedness : eating up my people as if they would eat bread ? * they háve not | called up-|on | God."

6 They were afráid where | no fear | was : for God hath broken the bones of him that besieged thee ; * thou hast put them to confusion, because Gód | hath de-|spised | them.

Its issue.

7 Oh that the salvation were given unto Ísrael | out of | Sion : Oh that the Lord would delíver his | people | out of capt-|ivity!

8 Thén should | Jacob re-|joice : ánd | Israel should be | right | glad.

## PSALM LIV. *Deus, in nomine.*

SAVE me O Gód, for thy | Name's | sake : ánd a-|venge me | in thy | strength.

Prayer in peril.

2 Héar my | prayer, O | God : and hearken únto the | words | of my | mouth.

3 For strangers are rísen | up a-|gainst me : and

tyrants which have not God before their éyes, | seek |
after my | soul.

4 Behold, Gód | is my | helper : the Lord is with  Confi-
thém | that up-|hold my | soul.          dence.

5 He shall reward évil | unto mine | enemies : de-
stróy thou | them | in thy | truth.

6 An offering of a free heart will I give thee, and  Gratitude.
praíse thy | Name, O | Lord : bé-|cause it | is so |
comfortable.

7 For he hath delivered me oút of | all my | trou-
ble : and mine eye hath séen his de-|sire up-|on mine|
enemies.


## PSALM LV. *Exaudi, Deus.*

HÉAR my | prayer, O | God : and híde not thy-|  Prayer in
self from | my pe-|tition.          peril.

2 Take héed unto | me, and | hear me : how I
moúrn in my | prayer, | and am | vexed.

3 The enemy crieth so, * and the ungodly cómeth |
on so | fast : for they are minded to do me some
mischief; * so malíciously | are they | set a-|gainst
me.

4 My heart is disquíet-|ed with-|in me : and the
féar of | death is | fallen up-|on me.

5 Fearfulness and trémbling are | come up-|on me :
and an horrible dréad hath | over-|whelmed | me.

6 And I said, O that I had wíngs | like a | dove :
for then would I flée a-|way, and | be at | rest.

7 Lo, then would I gét me a-|way far | off : ánd
re-|main | in the | wilderness.

8 I would make háste | to es-|cape : becaúse of
the | stormy | wind and | tempest.

9 Destroy their tongues O Lórd, | and di-|vide
them : for I have spied unríghteousness and | strife |
in the | city.

10 Day and night they go about withín the | walls
there-|of : mischief also and sórrow are | in the |
midst of | it.

11 Wíckedness | is there-|in : deceit and guíle | go
not | out of their | streets.

12 For it is not an open enemy that hath dóne
me | this dis-|honour : fór | then I | could have |
borne it.

13 Neither was it mine adversary that did mágnify
him-|self a-|gainst me : for then peradventure I wóuld
have | hid my-|self | from him.

14 But it was even thóu, | my com-|panion : my
guíde, and mine | own fam-|iliar | friend.

15 We tóok sweet | counsel to-|gether : and wálked
in the | house of | God as | friends.

16 Let death come hastily upon them, * and let
them go down quíck | into | hell : for wickedness ís
in their | dwellings, | and a-|mong them.

17 As for me, Í will | call upon | God : ánd the |
Lord | shall | save me.

18 In the evening and morning and at noon-day
will I práy, and | that | instantly : ánd | he shall |
hear my | voice.

19 It is he that hath delivered my soul in peace
from the báttle that | was a-|gainst me : fór | there
were | many | with me.

Punish-
ment in-
voked on
treacher-
ous ene-
mies.

The confi-
dence of
him who
trusts in
God.

20 Yea even God that endureth for ever * shall
héar me, and | bring them | down : for they wíll not |
turn, * nor | fear | God.

21 He laid his hands upon such as bé at | peace
with | him : ánd he | brake | his | covenant.

22 The words of his mouth were softer than butter, *
having | war in his | heart : his words were smoother
than oil, * and yét | be they | very | swords.

23 O cast thy burden upon the Lord, * and hé
shall | nourish | thee : and shall not súffer the | right-
eous to | fall for | ever.

24 Ánd | as for | them : thou O God shalt bring
them ínto the | pit | of de-|struction.

25 The blood-thirsty and deceitful men shall not
live óut | half their | days : nevertheless, my trúst
shall | be in | thee, O | Lord.


𝔐orning 𝔓rayer.


PSALM LVI.   *Miserere mei, Deus.*

BE merciful unto me O God, for man góeth a-|bout  Prayer
to de-|vour me : he is dáily | fighting, and |  amidst
enemies.
troubling | me.

2 Mine enemies are daily in hánd to | swallow me |
up : for they be many that fíght against | me, O |
thou most | Highest.


3 Nevertheless, thóugh I am | sometime a-|fraid :  Trust.
yét put | I my | trust in | thee.

4 I will praise Gód, be-|cause of his | word : I

have put my trust in God, * and will not féar what |
flesh can | do unto | me.

5 They daíly mis-|take my | words : all that they   Persecu-
imágine | is to | do me | evil.                 tion.

6 They hold all togéther, and | keep themselves |
close : and mark my steps, * whén they lay | wait |
for my | soul.

7 Shall they escápe | for their | wickedness : thou
O God in thý dis-|pleasure shalt | cast them | down.

8 Thou tellest my flittings; * put my téars | into
thy | bottle : are not thése things | noted | in thy |
book ?

9 Whensoever I call upon thee, then shall mine   Trust.
énemies be | put to | flight : this I knów; for | God
is | on my | side.

10 In God's wórd will | I re-|joice : in the Lórd's
word | will I | comfort | me.

11 Yea in Gód have I | put my | trust : I will not
be afráid what | man can | do unto | me.

12 Unto thee O Gód, will I | pay my | vows :   Thanks-
únto | thee will | I give | thanks.                    giving for
                                              deliver-
13 For thou hast delivered my soul from déath *   ance.
and my | feet from | falling : that I may walk before
Gód in the | light | of the | living.

## PSALM LVII. *Miserere mei, Deus.*

B E merciful unto me O God, be merciful unto me, *   Prayer in
   for my sóul | trusteth in | thee : and under the   danger.

shadow of thy wings shall be my refuge, * until this | tyranny be | over-|past.

2 I will cáll unto the | most high | God : even unto the God that shall perform the cáuse | which I | have in | hand.

3 Hé shall | send from | heaven : and save me from the reproof of hím | that would | eat me | up.

4 God shall send fórth his | mercy and | truth : my sóul | is a-|mong | lions.

5 And I lie even among the children of mén, that are | set on | fire : whose teeth are spears and arrows, * ánd their | tongue a | sharp | sword.

6 *Set up thyself O Gód, a-|bove the | heavens : and thy glóry a-|bove | all the | earth.*

7 They have laid a net for my feet, * and préssed | down my | soul : they have digged a pit before me, * and are fallen ínto the | midst of | it them-|selves.

Thanks- giving for deliver- ance.

8 My heart is fixed O Gód, my | heart is | fixed : Í will | sing, and | give | praise.

9 Awake up my glory; awáke, | lute and | harp : I mysélf | will a-|wake right | early.

10 I will give thanks unto thee O Lórd, a-|mong the | people : and I will síng unto | thee a-|mong the | nations.

11 For the greatness of thy mercy réacheth | unto the | heavens : ánd thy | truth | unto the | clouds.

12 *Set up thyself O Gód, a-|bove the | heavens : and thy glóry a-|bove | all the | earth.*

## PSALM LVIII. *Si vere utique.*

ARE your minds set upon righteousness, Ó ye | con-greg-|ation : and do ye judge the thing that is right, | O ye | sons of | men ?

Complaint against un- righteous- ness.

2 Yea, ye imagine mischief in your héart up-|on the | earth : ánd your | hands | deal with | wickedness.

3 The ungodly are froward, even fróm their | mother's | womb : as soon as they are born, they gó a-| stray, and | speak | lies.  *Character of the wicked.*

4 They are as venomous as the poíson | of a | serpent : even like the déaf | adder that | stoppeth her| ears ;

5 Which refuseth to hear the voíce | of the | charmer : chárm | he | never so | wisely.

6 Break their teeth O Gód | in their | mouths : smite the jáwbones | of the | lions, O | Lord.  *Their destruction invoked,*

Let them fall away like wáter that | runneth a-|pace : and when they shoot their árrows | let them be | rooted | out.

7 Let them consume away like a snail, and be like the untimely frúit | of a | woman : ánd | let them not | see the | sun.

8 Or ever your póts be made | hot with | thorns : so let indignation vex him, éven as a | thing | that is | raw.

9 The righteous shall rejoíce when he | seeth the | vengeance : he shall wash his footsteps ín the | blood | of the un-|godly.  *for the satisfaction of the righteous.*

10 So that a man shall say, Verily there is a rewárd | for the | righteous : doubtless there ís a | God that | judgeth the | earth.

### Ebening Prayer.

## PSALM LIX. *Eripe me de inimicis.*

DELIVER me from mine énemies, | O | God :
defend me from thém that | rise | up a-|gainst
me.

Prayer against the malice and power of enemies

2 O deliver me fróm the | wicked | doers : and
sáve me | from the | blood-thirsty | men.

3 For lo, they lie waiting | for my | soul : the
mighty men are gathered against me, * without any
offénce or | fault of | me, O | Lord.

4 They run and prepare themsélves with-|out my |
fault : arise thou thérefore to | help me, | and be-|
hold.

5 Stand up O Lord God of hosts, thou God of Is-
rael * to vísit | all the | heathen : and be not merciful
unto them that offénd | of mal-|icious | wickedness.

6 *They go to and fró | in the | evening : they grin
like a dog, and rún a-|bout | through the | city.*

7 Behold they speak with their mouth, * and swórds
are | in their | lips : fór | who | doth | hear ?

8 But thou O Lord shalt háve them | in de-|rision :
and thou shalt laúgh | all the | heathen to | scorn.

Trust.

9 *My strength will I ascríbe | unto | thee : for thóu
art the | God | of my | refuge.*

10 God shéweth me his | goodness | plenteously :
and God shall let me sée my de-|sire up-|on mine |
enemies.

Prayer repeated in faith.

11 Slay them not, lést my | people for-|get it : but
scatter them abroad among the people, and put them
dówn, * O | Lord, | our de-|fence.

12 For the sin of their mouth and for the words of their lips, * they shall be táken | in their | pride : and why? their préaching | is of | cursing and | lies.

13 Consume them in thy wrath, consúme them that | they may | perish : and know that it is God that ruleth in Jacob, * and únto the | ends | of the | world.

14 *And in the évening they | will re-|turn : grin like a dóg, and will | go a-|bout the | city.*

15 They will run hére and | there for | meat : and grúdge | if they | be not | satisfied.

16 As for me, I will sing of thy power * and will praise thy mercy betímes | in the | morning : for thou hast been my defence * and réfuge in the | day | of my | trouble.    Thanksgiving.

17 *Unto thee O my stréngth, | will I | sing : for thou O God art my réfuge, | and my | merciful | God.*

## PSALM LX.    *Deus, repulisti nos.*

O GOD thou hast cast us out, and scáttered | us a-|broad : thou hast also been displeased ; O túrn thee | unto | us a-|gain.    Desolation with the remembrance of past deliverance.

2 Thou hast moved the lánd, and di-|vided | it : heal the sóres there-|of, | for it | shaketh.

3 Thou hast shewed thy péople | heavy | things : thou hast gíven us a | drink of | deadly | wine.

4 Thou hast given a tóken for | such as | fear thee : that they may tríumph be-|cause | of the | truth.

5 Therefore were thý be-|loved de-|livered : hélp me with | thy right | hand, and | hear me.

6 God hath spoken in his holiness, "I will rejóce, and di-|vide | Sichem : and méte | out the | valley of | Succoth.    An ancient hymn of triumph.

7 "Gilead is mine, and Ma-|nasses is | mine :
Ephraim also is the strength of my héad; * | Judah |
is my | law-giver ;

8 "Moab is my wash-pot ; * over Edom will I cást |
out my | shoe : Philístia, | be thou | glad of | me."

9 Who will lead me ínto the | strong | city : whó  *Prayer in
will | bring me | into | Edom ?  *present need.*

10 Hast not thou cást us | out, O | God : wilt not
thou O Gód, go | out | with our | hosts ?

11 O be thóu our | help in | trouble : for váin | is
the | help of | man.

12 Through Gód will we | do great | acts : for it is
hé that shall | tread | down our | enemies.

## PSALM LXI. *Exaudi, Deus.*

HÉAR my | crying, O | God : gíve | ear | unto  *Prayer for*
my | prayer.  *safety,*

2 From the ends of the eárth will I | call upon |
thee : whén my | heart | is in | heaviness.

3 O set me up upon the róck that is | higher than |
I : for thou hast been my hope, and a strong tówer
for | me a-|gainst the | enemy.

4 I will dwell in thy tábern-|acle for | ever : and
my trust shall be únder the | covering | of thy |
wings.

5 For thou O Lord hast héard | my de-|sires : and  *resting on*
hast given an heritage únto | those that | fear thy |  *past help.*
Name.

6 Thou shalt grant the Kíng a | long | life : that
his years may endúre throughout | all | gener-|ations.

7 He shall dwéll before | God for | ever **:** O pre-
pare thy loving mercy and faithfulness, | that they |
may pre-|serve him.

8 So will I alway sing práise | unto thy | Name **:**
thát I may | daily per-|form my | vows.

### Morning Prayer.

### PSALM LXII. *Nonne Deo?*

M Y soul truly waiteth | still upon | God **:** for of
    him | cometh | my sal-|vation.
    2 *He verily is my stréngth and | my sal-|vation :* he
*is my defénce, só that I | shall not | greatly | fall.*
    3 How long will ye imagine mischief against |
every | man **:** ye shall be slain all the sort of you; *
yea as a tottering wall shall ye bé, and | like a | bro-
ken | hedge.
    4 Their device is only how to put him out whom
Gód | will ex-|alt **:** their delight is in lies; * they give
good words with their moúth, but | curse | with their |
heart.

Trust in
God in
spite of
enemies.

    5 Nevertheless my soul, waít thou | still upon |
God **:** fór my | hope | is in | him.
    6 *He truly is my stréngth and | my sal-|vation :* he
*is my defénce, | so·that I | shall not | fall.*
    7 In God is my heálth, | and my | glory **:** the rock
of my míght, and in | God | is my | trust.
    8 O put your trust in hím | alway, ye | people **:**
pour out your hearts befóre him * for | God | is our |
hope.

Trust in
God from
experi-
ence.

    9 As for the children of mén, they | are but | va-
nity **:** the children of men are deceitful upon the

Man's
power fails
before

weights, * they are altogether líghter than | vani-|ty it-|self.

God's judgment.

10 O trust not in wrong and robbery, * give not yoursélves | unto | vanity : if riches íncrease, | set not your | heart up-|on them.

11 God spake once, * and twice I have álso | heard the | same : that pówer be-|longeth | unto | God;

12 And that thóu, | Lord, art | merciful : for thou rewardest every mán ac-|cording | to his | work.


## PSALM LXIII.    *Deus, Deus meus.*

O GOD, thou art my God, éarly will I | seek | thee : 2 My soul thirsteth for thee, my flesh also long- eth after thee, * in a barren and a dry lánd | where no | water | is.

The soul's desire for God.

3 Thus have I lóoked for | thee in | holiness : that I míght be-|hold thy | power and | glory.


4 For thy loving-kindness is bétter than the | life it-|self : mý | lips | shall | praise thee.

Blessed-ness of fellowship with Him.

5 As long as I live will I magnify thée | on this | manner : and líft up my | hands in | thy | Name.

6 My soul shall be satisfied, even as it wére with | marrow and | fatness : when my mouth práiseth | thee with | joyful | lips.

7 Have I not remembered thée | in my | bed : and thought upon thée | when | I was | waking?

8 Becáuse thou hast | been my | helper : therefore under the shádow of thy | wings will | I re-|joice.

9 My sóul | hangeth up-|on thee : thy right hánd | hath up-|holden | me.

10 These also that seek the húrt | of my | soul :    His sure
théy shall | go | under the | earth.             judgment.

11 Let them fall upon the édge | of the | sword :
that théy may | be a | portion for | foxes.

12 But the King shall rejoice in God; * all they
also that swear by hím shall | be com-|mended : for
the mouth of thém that speak | lies | shall be |
stopped.

## PSALM LXIV. *Exaudi, Deus.*

HEAR my voice O Gód, | in my | prayer : pre-    Prayer
serve my life from | fear | of the | enemy.        against
                                              enemies.
2 Hide me from the gathering togéther | of the |
froward : and from the ínsur-|rection of | wicked |
doers ;

3 Who have whet their tóngue | like a | sword :
and shoot out their árrows, | even | bitter | words ;

4 That they may privily shoot at hím | that is |
perfect : suddenly dó they | hit him, | and | fear not.

5 They encóurage them-|selves in | mischief : and
commune among themselves how they may lay snares, *
and sáy, that | no man | shall | see them.

6 They imagine wíckedness and | practise | it : that
they keep secret among themselves, every man in the |
deep | of his | heart.

7 But God shall suddenly shoot at them wíth a |    Judgment
swift | arrow : thát | they | shall be | wounded.      executed
                                              upon
8 Yea, their own tóngues shall | make them | fall :    them.
insomuch thát whoso séeth them shall | laugh | them
to | scorn.

9 And all men that see it shall say, * Thís hath |

God | done : for they shall percéive that | it is | his | work.

10 The righteous shall rejoice in the Lord, and pút his | trust in | him : and all they that are trúe of | heart | shall be | glad.

## Ebening Praper.

### PSALM LXV. *Te decet hymnus.*

THOU O Gód, art | praised in | Sion : and unto thee shall the vów be per-|formed | in Je-| rusalem.

2 Thóu that | hearest the | prayer : únto | thee shall | all flesh | come.

3 My misdéeds pre-|vail a-|gainst me : Ó be thou | merciful | unto our | sins.

4 Blessed is the man whom thou choosest and recéivest | unto | thee : he shall dwell in thy court, * and shall be satisfied with the pleasures of thy house, * éven | of thy | holy | temple.

Thanksgiving to God for personal mercy;

5 Thou shalt shew us wonderful things in thy right-eousness, * O Gód of | our sal-|vation : thou that art the hope of all the ends of the earth, * and of them thát re-|main in the | broad | sea.

for His government of the world;

6 Who in his strength sétteth | fast the | mountains : ánd is | girded a-|bout with | power.

7 Who stilleth the ráging | of the | sea : and the noise of his wáves, and the | madness | of the | people.

8 They also that dwell in the uttermost parts of the earth shall be afráid | at thy | tokens : thou that makest the outgoings of the mórning and | evening to | praise | thee.

9 Thou visitest the eárth, and | blessest | it : thóu | for the fruitful seasons.
makest it | very | plenteous.

10 The river of Gód is | full of | water : thou
preparest their corn, for só thou pro-|videst | for the |
earth.

11 Thou waterest her furrows, * thou sendest rain
into the líttle | valleys there-|of : thou makest it soft
with the drops of ráin, * and | blessest the | increase |
of it.

12 Thou crownest the yéar | with thy | goodness :
ánd thy | clouds | drop | fatness.

13 They shall drop upon the dwéllings | of the |
wilderness : and the little hílls shall re-|joice on |
every | side.

14 The fólds shall be | full of | sheep : the valleys
also shall stand so thick with córn, * that | they shall |
laugh and | sing.


## PSALM LXVI. *Jubilate Deo.*

O BE joyful in Gód, | all ye | lands : sing praises Call to universal praise of God;
unto the honour of his Name, máke his | praise |
to be | glorious.

2 Say unto God, O how wonderful árt thou | in thy |
works : through the greatness of thy power shall thine
enemies be foúnd | liars | unto | thee.

3 For all the wórld shall | worship | thee : síng of |
thee, * and | praise thy | Name.

4 O come hither, and behóld the | works of | God : for His wonders;
how wonderful he is in his dóing | toward the | chil-
dren of | men.

5 He turned the séa into | dry | land : so that they

went through the water on foot; * thére did | we re-|
joice there-|of.

6 He ruleth with his power for ever ; * his éyes be-|
hold the | people : and such as will not believe shall
not be áble | to ex-|alt them-|selves.

7 O práise our | God, ye | people : and make the for His
discipline.
vóice of his | praise | to be | heard ;

8 Who hóldeth our | soul in | life : and súffereth |
not our | feet to | slip.

9 For thou O Gód, hast | proved | us : thou also
hast tríed us, | like as | silver is | tried.

10 Thou bróughtest us | into the | snare : and láid-
est | trouble up-|on our | loins.

11 Thou sufferedst men to ríde | over our | heads :
we went through fire and water, * and thou broughtest
us óut | into a | wealthy | place.

12 I will go into thine hóuse | with burnt-|offerings : Personal
acknow-
and will pay thee my vows, * which I promised with ledgment
of His
my lips * and spake with my móuth, | when I | was goodness.
in | trouble.

13 I will offer unto thee fat burnt-sacrifices, * wíth
the | incense of | rams : Í will | offer | bullocks and |
goats.

14 O come hither and hearken, * all yé that | fear |
God : and I will tell you what hé hath | done | for
my | soul.

15 I called unto hím | with my | mouth : and gáve
him | praises | with my | tongue.

16 If I incline unto wíckedness | with mine | heart :
thé | Lord | will not | hear me.

17 Bút | God hath | heard me : and consídered the | voice | of my | prayer.

18 Praised be God who hath not cást | out my | prayer : nór | turned his | mercy | from me.

### PSALM LXVII. *Deus misereatur.*

G OD be merciful únto | us, and | bless us : and
shew us the light of his countenance, ánd be |
merciful | unto | us ;

*Prayer and praise for blessings future and past.*

2 That thy wáy may be | known upon | earth : thy sáving | health a-|mong all | nations.

3 *Let the people práise | thee, O | God : yéa, let | all the | people | praise thee.*

4 O let the nations rejóice | and be | glad : for thou shalt judge the folk righteously, * and góvern the | nations up-|on | earth.

5 *Let the people práise | thee, O | God : lét | all the | people | praise thee.*

6 Then shall the éarth bring | forth her | increase : and God even our own Gód, shall | give | us his | blessing.

7 Gód | shall | bless us : and all the énds of the | world shall | fear | him.

### Morning Prayer.

### PSALM LXVIII. *Exurgat Deus.*

L ET God arise, and let his énem-|ies be | scattered :
let them álso that | hate him | flee be-|fore
him.

*The praise of God the Ruler of the world.*

2 Like as the smoke vanisheth, so shalt thou drive |

them a-|way : and like as wax melteth at the fire, *
so let the ungodly pérish | at the | presence of |
God.

3 But let the righteous be glád and re-|joice before |
God : lét them | also be | merry and | joyful.

4 O sing unto God, and sing práises | unto his |
Name : magnify him that rideth upon the heavens as
it were upon an horse; * praise him in his Name
JÁH, | and re-|joice be-|fore him.

5 He is a Father of the fatherless, and defendeth
the cáuse | of the | wídows : even Gód in his | holy |
habit-|ation.

6 He is the God that maketh men to be of one mind
in an house, * and bringeth the prísoners | out of capt-|
ivity : but letteth the rúnagates con-|tinue | in |
scarceness.

7 O God, when thou wentest fórth be-|fore the |
people : whén thou | wentest | through the | wilder-
ness,

8 The earth shook, * and the heavens drópped at
the | presence of | God : even as Sinai also was
moved at the presence of God, who ís the | God of |
Isra-|el.

9 Thou O God sentest a gracious ráin upon | thine
in-|heritance : and refréshedst it | when | it was |
weary.

10 Thy congregátion shall | dwell there-|in : for
thou O God hast of thy góodness pre-|pared | for the |
poor.

11 The Lórd | gave the | word : gréat was the |
·company | of the | preachers.

His care
for His
people
in the
wilder-
ness;

in the con-
quest of
Canaan;

12 Kings with their armies did flée, and | were dis-|
comfited : and théy of the | household di-|vided the |
spoil.

13 Though ye have lien among the pots, * yet
shall ye be as the wíngs | of a | dove : that is covered
with sílver wings, | * and her | feathers like | gold.

14 When the Almighty scattered kíngs | for their |
sake : then were théy as | white as | snow in |
Salmon.

15 As the hill of Basan, só is | God's | hill : even   in the
an hígh hill, | as the | hill of | Basan.       entrance
                                             into Sion.
16   Why hop ye so ye high hills ? * this is God's
hill, in the which it pléaseth | him to | dwell : yea the
Lórd will a-|bide in | it for | ever.

17 The chariots of God are twenty thousand,
éven | thousands of | angels : and the Lord is among
them, as ín the | holy | place of | Sinai.

18 Thou art gone up on high, thou hast led captivity
captive, * and receíved | gifts for | men : yea even for
thine enemies, that the Lórd | God might | dwell a-|
mong them.

———————

19 Praised bé the | Lord | daily : even the God   Praise of
who helpeth us, and póureth his | bene-|fits up-|on   God the
                                                     Con-
us.                                                       queror.

20 He is our God, even the God of whóm | cometh
sal-|vation : God is the Lórd, by | whom we es-|
cape | death.

21 God shall wound the héad | of his | enemies :
and the hairy scalp of such a one as góeth on | still |
in his | wickedness.

22 The Lord hath said, "I will bring my people again, as I | did from | Basan : mine own will I bring again, as I did sometime fróm the | deep | of the | sea.

23 That thy foot may be dipped in the blóod | of thine | enemies : and that the tongue of thy dógs may be | red | through the | same."

———————

24 It is well seen O Gód, | how thou | goest : how thou my God and Kíng, | goest | in the | sanctuary. *The entrance of God into the sanctuary.*

25 The singers go before, the mínstrels | follow | after : in the midst are the dámsels | playing | with the | timbrels.

26 Give thanks O Israel unto God the Lórd in the | congreg-|ations : fróm the | ground | of the | heart.

27 There is little Benjamin their ruler, * and the prínces of | Judah their | counsel : the princes of Zá-bulon, | and the | princes of | Nephthali.

28 Thy God hath sént forth | strength for | thee : stablish the thing O Gód, that | thou hast | wrought in | us, *The future glory of Israel.*

29 For thy temple's sáke | at Je-|rusalem : so shall kíngs bring | presents | unto | thee.

30 When the company of the spear-men, and multitude of the mighty are scattered abroad among the beasts of the people, * so that they húmbly bring | pieces of | silver : and when he hath scattered the péople | that de-|light in | war ;

31 Then shall the princes cóme | out of | Egypt : the Morians' land shall soon stretch oút her | hands | unto | God.

32 Sing unto God, O ye kíngdoms | of the | earth : The universal dominion of God in the future.
Ó sing | praises | unto the | Lord;

33 Who sitteth in the heavens over áll | from the be-|ginning : lo he doth send out his voice, yéa, and | that a | mighty | voice.

34 Ascribe ye the power to Gód over | Isra-|el : his wórship, and | strength is | in the | clouds.

35 O God, wonderful art thóu in thy | holy | places : even the God of Israel; * he will give strength and power unto his péople; | * blessed | be | God.

## Ebening Prayer.

### PSALM LXIX. *Salvum me fac.*

SÁVE | me, O | God : for the waters are come A lamentation in sore distress,
ín, | even | unto my | soul.

2 I stick fast in the deep mire, whére no | ground | is : I am come into deep waters, * só that the | floods run | over | me.

3 I am weary of crýing my | throat is | dry : my sight faileth me for wáiting so | long up-|on my | God.

4 They that hate me without a cause are móre than the | hairs of my | head : they that are mine enemies ánd would de-|stroy me | guiltless, are | mighty.

5 I paid them the thíngs that I | never | took : God thou knowest my simpleness, * ánd my | faults are not | hid from | thee.

6 Let not them that trust in thee O Lord God of hosts, be ashámed | for my | cause : let not those that seek thee be confounded through me, * O Lórd | God of | Isra-|el.

7 And why? for thy sake háve I | suffered re-| due to zeal for righteous-ness.
proof : sh-|ame hath | covered my | face.

8 I am become a stránger | unto my | brethren :
even an álien | unto my | mother's | children.

9 For the zeal of thine house hath éven | eaten |
me : and the rebukes of them that rebuked thée are |
fallen up-|on | me.

10 I wept, and chástened my-|self with | fasting :
and thát was | turned to | my re-|proof.

11 I put ón | sackcloth | also : ánd they | jested
up-|on | me.

12 They that sit in the gáte | speak a-|gainst me :
ánd the | drunkards make | songs up-|on me.


13 But Lord I make my práyer | unto | thee : ín | Prayer in this ex-tremity,
an ac-|ceptable | time.

14 Hear me O God in the múltitude | of thy |
mercy : even ín the | truth of | thy sal-|vation.

15 Take me out of the míre, | that I | sink not :
O let me be delivered from them that háte me and |
out of the | deep | waters.

16 Let not the water-flood drown me, * neither let
the déep | swallow me | up : and let not the pít | shut
her | mouth up-|on me.

17 Hear me O Lord, for thy lóving-|kindness is |
comfortable : turn thee unto me accórding to the |
multitude | of thy | mercies.

18 And hide not thy face from thy servant, fór
I | am in | trouble : Ó | haste | thee, and | hear
me.

19 Draw nigh únto my | soul, and | save it : O de-
líver me, be-|cause of | mine | enemies.

20 Thou hast known my reproof, my sháme, and |

15

my dis-|honour : mine ádversaries are | all in | thy | sight.

21 Thy rebuke hath broken my héart; I am | full of | heaviness : I looked for some to have pity on me, but there was no man, * neither fóund I | any to | comfort | me.

22 They gáve me | gall to | eat : and when I was thirsty they gáve me | vine-|gar to | drink.

23 Let their table be made a snare to táke them-| selves with-|al : and let the things that should have been for their wealth be unto thém | an oc-|casion of | falling. *and denunciation of enemies.*

24 Let their eyes be blínded, | that they | see not : and éver | bow thou | down their | backs.

25 Pour out thine Índig-|nation up-|on them : and let thy wráthful dis-|pleasure take | hold of | them.

26 Let their hábit-|ation be | void : and nó man to | dwell | in their | tents.

27 For they persecute hím whom | thou hast | smitten : and they talk how they may véx | them whom | thou hast | wounded.

28 Let them fall from óne wickedness | to an-|other : ánd | not come | into thy | righteousness.

29 Let them be wiped out of the bóok | of the | living : and nót be | written a-|mong the | righteous.

30 As for me, when I am póor | and in | heavi-ness : thy hélp, O | God, shall | lift me | up. *Thanksgiving.*

31 I will praise the Name of Gód | with a | song : and mágni-|fy it with | thanks-|giving.

32 This álso shall | please the | Lord : better than a búllock | that hath | horns and | hoofs.

33 The humble shall consider thís, | and be | glad :
seek ye after Gód, | and your | soul shall | live.

34 For the Lórd | heareth the | poor : ánd de-|
spiseth | not his | prisoners.

35 Let héaven and | earth | praise him : the séa,
and | all that | moveth there-|in.

36 For God will save Sion, * and búild the | cities
of | Judah : that men may dwéll there, and | have it |
in pos-|session.

37 The posterity also of his servants sháll in-|
herit | it : and they that lóve his | Name shall | dwell
there-|in.


## PSALM LXX. *Deus in adjutorium.*

### (Compare Ps. xl. 16—21.)

HASTE thee O Gód, to de-|liver | me : make
háste to | help | me, O | Lord.

2 Let them be ashamed and confounded that séek |
after my | soul : let them be turned backward and pút
to con-|fusion that | wish me | evil.

3 Let them for their reward be sóon | brought to |
shame : that crý | over me, | " There, | there."

4 But let all those that seek thee be jóyful and |
glad in | thee : and let all such as delight in thy salva-
tion say álway, * "The | Lord | be | praised."

5 As for me, I am póor | and in | misery : háste
thee | unto | me, O | God.

6 Thou art my hélper, and | my red-|eemer : O
Lórd, | make no | long | tarrying.

Prayer in
distress.

**Morning Prayer.**

## PSALM LXXI. *In te, Domine, speravi.*

IN thee O Lord háve I | put my | trust : let me
néver be | put | to con-|fusion. <sub></sub>Prayer of personal trust,

But rid me and delíver me | in thy | righteous-
ness : incline thine éar | unto | me, and | save me.

2 Be thou my strong hold, whereuntó I may | alway
re-|sort : thou hast promised to help me, * for thou
art my hóuse of de-|fence, | and my | castle.

3 Deliver me O my God out of the hánd of | the
un-|godly : out of the hánd of the un-|righteous and |
cruel | man.

4 For thou O Lord God art the thíng | that I |
long for : thou art my hópe, | even | from my |
youth.

5 Through thee have I been holden up ever sínce |
I was | born : thou art he that took me out of my
mother's womb ; * my práise | shall be | always of |
thee.

6 I am become as it were a mónster | unto | many : <sub></sub>in distress and per-secution.
but my súre | trust | is in | thee.

7 O let my mouth be fílled | with thy | praise :
that I may sing of thy glóry and | honour | all the
day | long.

8 Cast me not awáy in the | time of | age : forsake
me not whén my | strength | faileth | me.

9 For mine énemies | speak a-|gainst me : and they
that lay wait for my soul táke their | counsel to-|
gether, | saying

"Gód hath for-|saken | him : persecute him and
take him, for there is nóne | to de-|liver | him."

10 Go not fár from | me, O | God : my Gód, | haste | thee to | help me.

11 Let them be confounded and perish that áre a-|gainst my | soul : let them be covered with shame and dishónour that | seek to | do me | evil. Con-fidence.

12 As for me, I will pátiently a-|bide | alway : ánd will | praise thee | more and | more.

13 My mouth shall daily speak of thy ríghteous-ness | and sal-|vation : fór I | know no | end there-|of.

14 I will go forth in the stréngth of the | Lord | God : and will make méntion | of thy | righteousness | only.

15 Thou O God hast taught me from my yóuth up | until | now : therefore will I téll | of thy | won-drous | works.

16 Forsake me not O God in mine old age, whén I am | gray-|headed : until I have shewed thy strength unto this generation, * and thy power to all thém that are | yet | for to | come.

17 Thy righteousness O Gód, is | very | high : and great things are they that thou hast done ; * O Gód, | who is | like unto | thee ? Divine discipline.

18 O what great troubles and adversities hast thou shewed me ! * and yet didst thou túrn | and re-|fresh me : yea and broughtest me from the déep | of the | earth a-|gain.

19 Thou hast bróught me to | great | honour : and cómforted | me on | every | side.

20 Therefore will I praise thee and thy faithfulness O God, * playing upon an ínstru-|ment of | musick : Thanks-giving.

unto thee will I sing upon the harp, * O thou Hóly |
One of | Isra-|el.

21 My lips will be fain when I síng | unto | thee :
and so will my sóul | whom thou | hast de-|livered.

22 My tongue also shall talk of thy ríghteous-
ness | all the day | long : for they are confounded and
brought unto sháme that | seek to | do me | evil.


## PSALM LXXII. *Deus, judicium.*

G IVE the Kíng thy | judgements, O | God : and
  thy ríghteousness | unto the | King's | son.

*The character of the Divine Kingdom*

2 Then shall he judge thy people accórding | unto |
right : ánd de-|fend | the | poor.

3 The mountains álso shall | bring | peace : and the
little hílls | righteousness | unto the | people.

4 He shall keep the simple fólk | by their | right :
defend the children of the póor, * and | punish the |
wrong | doer.

5 They shall fear thee, as long as the sún and |
moon en-|dureth : from óne gener-|ation | to an-|
other.

*everlasting:*

6 He shall come down like the ráin into a | fleece
of | wool : éven as the | drops that | water the |
earth.

7 In his tíme shall the | righteous | flourish : yea
and abundance of péace, so | long as the | moon en-|
dureth.

8 His dominion shall be also from the óne sea | to
the | other : and from the flóod | unto the | world's |
end.

*universal:*

9 They that dwell in the wilderness shall | kneel be-|fore him : his énem-|ies shall | lick the | dust.

10 The kings of Tharsis and of the ísles shall | give | presents : the kings of Arábia and | Saba shall| bring | gifts.

11 All kings shall fáll | down be-|fore him : áll | nations shall | do him | service.

12 For he shall deliver the póor | when he | crieth : the needy álso, and | him that | hath no | helper.

based on mercy and righteous-ness:

13 He shall be favourable tó the | simple and | needy : and shall presérve the | souls | of the | poor.

14 He shall deliver their sóuls from | falsehood and | wrong : and déar shall their | blood be | in his | sight.

15 He shall live, and unto him shall be gíven of the | gold of A-|rabia : prayer shall be made ever unto hím, * and | daily shall | he be | praised.

16 There shall be an heap of corn in the earth, hígh up-|on the | hills : his fruit shall shake like Libanus, * and shall be green in the cíty like | grass up-|on the | earth.

crowned with out-ward and inward blessings.

17 His Name shall endure for ever ; * his Name shall remain under the sún a-|mong the post-|erities : which shall be blessed through hím ; * and | all the | heathen shall | praise him.

---

18 *Blessed be the Lord God, even the Gód of | Isra-| el : which ónly | doeth | wondrous | things ;*

19 *And blessed be the Name of his Májes-|ty for | ever : and all the earth shall be filled with his Májesty. | Amen, | A-|men.*

## PSALM LXXIII. *Quam bonus Israel!*

TRULY God is loving únto | Isra-|el : even unto súch as | are of a | clean | heart.

2 Nevertheless my féet were | almost | gone : mý | treadings had | well-nigh | slipt.

3 And why? I was gríeved | at the | wicked : I do also sée the un-|godly in | such pro-|sperity.

4 For they are in nó | peril of | death : bút are | lusty | and | strong.

5 They come in no misfórtune like | other | folk : neither áre they | plagued like | other | men.

6 And this is the cause that they are só | holden with | pride : ánd | over-|whelmed with | cruelty.

7 Their éyes | swell with | fatness : and they dó | even | what they | lust.

8 They corrupt other, and spéak of | wicked | blasphemy : their tálking is a-|gainst the | most | High.

9 For they stretch forth their móuth | unto the | heaven : and their tóngue | goeth | through the | world.

10 Therefore fall the péople | unto | them : and thereoút suck | they no | small ad-|vantage.

11 "Tush" say they, "hów should | God per-|ceive it : is there knówledge | in the | most | High?"

12 Lo these are the ungodly,*these prosper in the world, and these have ríches | in pos-|session : and I said, "Then have I cleansed my heart in váin,*and | washed mine | hands in | innocency."

13 All the day lóng have | I been | punished : ánd | chastened | every | morning.

14 Yea and I had almost sáid | even as | they : but

lo, then I should have condemned the géner-|ation | of
thy | children.

15 Then thought I to únder-|stand | this : bút it | The
was too | hard for | me,                               solution.

16 Until I went into the sánctuary | of | God :
then understóod I the | end of | these | men ;

17 Namely how thou dost sét them in | slippery |
places : and castest them dówn, | and de-|stroyest |
them.                                                        .

18 Oh, how súddenly do | they con-|sume : pérish,
and | come to a | fearful | end !

19 Yea even like as a dréam | when one a-|waketh :
so shalt thou make their ímage to | vanish | out of
the | city.

20 Thús my | heart was | grieved : and it wént |
even | through my | reins.

21 So fóolish was | I, and | ignorant : éven as it |
were a | beast be-|fore thee.


22 Nevertheléss, I am | alway by | thee : for thou  The sure
hast hólden me | by my | right | hand.              trust of the
                                                    righteous.
23 Thou shalt guíde me | with thy | counsel : and
after thát re-|ceive | me with | glory.

24 Whom have Í in | heaven but | thee : and
there is none upon earth that I desíre in com-|parison |
of | thee.

25 My flésh and my | heart | faileth : but God is
the strength of my héart, | and my | portion for |
ever.

26 For lo, they that forsáke | thee shall | perish :
thou hast destroyed all them that commít fornic-|ation
a-|gainst | thee.

27 But it is good for me to hold me fast by God, *

to put my trúst in the | Lord | God : and to speak of all thy works in the gátes | of the | daughter of | Sion.

## PSALM LXXIV. *Ut quid, Deus?*

O GOD, wherefore art thou ábsent from | us so | long : why is thy wrath so hot agáinst the | sheep | of thy | pasture?

2 O think upón thy | congreg-|ation : whom thou hast púrchased, | and red-|eemed of | old.

3 Think upon the tríbe of | thine in-|heritance : and mount Síon, where-|in | thou hast | dwelt.

4 Lift up thy feet, that thou mayest utterly de- stróy | every | enemy : which hath dóne | evil | in thy | sanctuary.

5 Thine adversaries roar in the mídst of thy | con- greg-|ations : and sét | up their | banners for | tokens.

6 He that hewed timber afore oút of the | thick | trees : was known to bríng it | to an | excellent | work.

7 But now they break down all the cárved | work there-|of : wíth | axes | and | hammers.

8 They have set fíre upon thy | holy | places : and have defiled the dwelling-place of thy Náme, | even | unto the | ground.

9 Yea they said in their hearts, "Let us make hávock of them | alto-|gether" : thus have they burnt up all the hóuses of | God | in the | land.

10 We see not our tokens, * there is not óne | pro- phet | more : no, not one is there among us, that únder-|standeth | any | more.

11 O God, how long shall the adversary dó | this dis-|honour : how long shall the énemy blas-|pheme thy | Name, for | ever ?

12 Why withdráwest | thou thy | hand : why pluck-est thou not thy right hand out of thy bósom | to con-|sume the | enemy ?

13 For Gód is my | King of | old : the help that is done upon eárth he | doeth | it him-|self.   God's help of old.

14 Thou didst divide the séa | through thy | power : thou brakest the héads of the | dragons | in the | waters.

15 Thou smotest the heads of Levía-|than in | pieces : and gavest him to be méat for the | people | in the | wilderness.

16 Thou broughtest out fountains and waters oút of the | hard | rocks : thóu | driedst up | mighty | waters.

17 The day is thíne, and the | night is | thine : thou hast prepáred the | light | and the | sun.

18 Thou hast set all the bórders | of the | earth : thóu hast | made | summer and | winter.

19 Remember this O Lord, how the énemy | hath re-|buked : and how the foolish péople | hath blas-| phemed thy | Name.   Remember us, O Lord.

20 O deliver not the soul of thy turtle-dove unto the múltitude | of the | enemies : and forget not the congregátion | of the | poor for | ever.

21 Lóok up-|on the | covenant : for all the earth is full of dárkness, and | cruel | habit-|ations.

22 O let not the simple gó a-|way a-|shamed : but let the poor and néedy give | praise | unto thy | Name.

23 Arise O God, maintain thine | own | cause : remember how the foolish mán blas-|phemeth | thee | daily.

24 Forget not the voice | of thine | enemies : the presumption of them that hate thee increáseth | ever | more and | more.

### Morning Prayer.

PSALM LXXV. *Confitebimur tibi.*

UNTO thee O Gód, do | we give | thanks : yeá, unto | thee do | we give | thanks.

Thanks-giving for

2 Thy Náme also | is so | nigh : and thát do thy | wondrous | works de-|clare.

3 "When I receíve the | congreg-|ation : I shall júdge ac-|cording | unto | right.

God's sentence of judgment,

4 "The earth is weak, and all the inhábit-|ers there-|of : Í bear | up the | pillars | of it.

5 "I said unto the fools, 'Déal | not so | madly': and to the ungódly, | 'Set not | up your | horn.'

6 "'Set not úp your | horn on | high : and spéak not | with a | stiff | neck.'"

7 For promotion cometh neither from the eást, nor | from the | west : nór | yet | from the | south.

which is executed in right-eousness.

8 And whý? | God is the | Judge : he putteth down óne, and | setteth | up an-|other.

9 For in the hand of the Lord there is a cúp, and the | wine is | red : it is full mixed, ánd he | poureth | out of the | same.

10 Ás for the | dregs there-|of : all the ungodly of the éarth shall | drink them, and | suck them | out.

11 But I will tálk of the | God of | Jacob : ánd | praise | him for | ever.

12 All the horns of the ungodly álso | will I | break : and the hórns of the | righteous shall | be ex-|alted.

## PSALM LXXVI. *Notus in Judæa.*

IN Jéwry is | God | known : his Náme is | great in | Isra-|el.    God the Deliverer of Israel.

2 At Sálem | is his | tabernacle : ánd his | dwell-ing | in | Sion.

3 There brake he the árrows | of the | bow : the shiéld, the | sword, | and the | battle.

4 Thou art of móre | honour and | might : thán the | hills | of the | robbers.    His victory.

5 The proud are robbed, théy have | slept their | sleep : and all the men whose hánds were | mighty have | found | nothing.

6 At thy rebúke, O | God of | Jacob : bóth the | chariot and | horse are | fallen.

7 Thou even thóu art | to be | feared : and who may stánd in thy | sight when | thou art | angry ?    He is an invincible Judge,

8 Thou didst cause thy júdgement to be | heard from | heaven : the eárth | trembled, | and was | still,

9 When Gód a-|rose to | judgement : and to hélp | all the | mcek upon | earth.

10 The fierceness of man shall túrn | to thy | praise : and the fiérceness of | them shalt | thou re-|frain.    to be feared of all men.

11 Promise unto the Lord your God and keep it,

all yé that are | round a-|bout him : bring presents
unto hím that | ought | to be | feared.

12 He shall refráin the | spirit of | princes : and is
wonderful amóng the | kings | of the | earth.


## PSALM LXXVII. *Voce mea ad Dominum.*

I WILL cry unto Gód | with my | voice : even
unto God will I cry with my voice, and hé shall |
hearken | unto | me.

2 In the time of my tróuble I | sought the | Lord :
my sore ran and ceased not in the night-seáson; *
my | soul re-|fused | comfort.

3 When I am in heaviness, Í wil! | think upon |
God : when my héart is | vexed, I | will com-|plain.

A cry
of the
afflicted in

4 Thou hóldest mine | eyes | waking : I am so feé-
ble, | that I | cannot | speak.

5 I have considered the | days of | old : ánd the |
years | that are | past.

6 I cáll to re-|membrance my | song : and in the
night I commune with mine own héart, * and | search |
out my | spirits.

the time
of self-
question-
ing, and

7 Will the Lord absént him-|self for | ever : and
will he | be no | more in-|treated ?

8 Is his mercy cléan | gone for | ever : and is his
promise come utterly tó an | end for | ever-|more ?

9 Hath God forgótten | to be | gracious : and will
he shut up his lóving-|kindness | in dis-|pleasure ?

apparent
desertion.

10 And I said, " Ít is mine | own in-|firmity : but
I will remember the years of the right hánd | of the |
most | Highest.

Comfort in
recalling
God's
works

11 "I will remember the wórks | of the | Lord : and call to mínd thy | wonders of | old | time.

12 "I will think álso of | all thy | works : and my tálking shall | be of | thy | doings."

13 Thy wáy, O | God, is | holy : who is so gréat a | God as | our | God?

14 Thou art the Gód that | doeth | wonders : and hast decláred thy | power a-|mong the | people.

15 Thou hast míghtily de-|livered thy | people : éven the | sons of | Jacob and | Joseph.

16 The waters saw thee O God,* the waters sáw thee, and | were a-|fraid : the dépths | also | were | troubled. *in the Exodus.*

17 The clouds poured out wáter, * the | air | thundered : ánd thine | arrows | went a-|broad.

18 The voice of thy thunder was héard | round a-|bout : the lightnings shone upon the ground;* the eárth was | moved, and | shook with-|al.

19 Thy way is in the sea, * and thy páths in the | great | waters : ánd thy | footsteps | are not | known.

20 Thou léddest thy | people like | sheep : bý the | hand of | Moses and | Aaron.

### Ebening Prayer.

PSALM LXXVIII.  *Attendite, popule.*

HEAR my láw, | O my | people : incline your ears únto the | words | of my | mouth. *The lessons of the providential history of Israel.*

2 I will open my móuth | in a | parable : I will decláre hard | senten-|ces of | old ;

3 Whích we have | heard and | known : and súch
as our | fathers have | told | us ;

4 That we should not hide them from the children
of the géner-|ations to | come : but to shew the honour
of the Lord, * his mighty and wónderful | works that |
he hath | done.

5 He made a covenant with Jacob, * and gave
Ísra-|el a | law : which he commanded óur fore-|
fathers * to | teach their | children ;

6 That their postéri-|ty might | know it : and the
chíldren | which were | yet un-|born ;

7 To the intent that whén | they came | up : théy
might | shew their | children the | same ;

8 That they might pút their | trust in | God : and
not to forget the works of God, * bút to | keep | his
com-|mandments ;

9 And not to be as their forefathers, * a faithless
and stúbborn | gener-|ation : a generation that set not
their heart aright, * and whose spirit cléaveth not | sted-
fastly | unto | God ;

10 Líke as the | children of | Ephraim : who being
harnessed and carrying bows, turned themselves báck |
in the | day of | battle.

11 They kept not the cóven-|ant of | God : and
wóuld not | walk | in his | law ;

12 But forgát what | he had | done : and the won-
derful wórks that | he had | shewed | for them.

13 Marvellous things did he in the sight of our fore-   The first
fathers, ín the | land of | Egypt : éven | in the | field   miracles
of | Zoan.   of the
                                                            Exodus.

14 He divided the sea, and lét | them go | through :
he made the wáters to | stand | on an | heap.

15 In the day-time also he léd them | with a | cloud :
and all the níght through | with a | light of | fire.

16 He clave the hard rócks | in the | wilderness :
and gave them drink thereof, as it had béen | out of
the | great | depth.

17 He brought waters oút of the | stony | rock : so
that it gúshed | out | like the | rivers.

18 Yet for all this they sínned | more a-|gainst  The mur-
him : and provóked the most | Highest | in the |  murings of
wilderness.                                           the people.

19 They tempted Gód | in their | hearts : and re-
quíred | meat | for their | lust.

20 They spake against Gód | also, | saying : "Shall
God prepáre a | table | in the | wilderness? "

21 "He smote the stony rock indeed that the water
gushed out, * and the stréams | flowed with-|al : but
can he give bread also, * or províde | flesh | for his |
people?"

22 When the Lord heard thís, | he was | wroth : so  Miraculous
the fire was kindled in Jacob, * and there came up  answer to
heavy displéasure a-|gainst | Isra-|el ;                the mur-
                                                        muring.

23 Because they beliéved | not in | God : and pút
not their | trust | in his | help.

24 So he commánded the | clouds a-|bove : ánd |
opened the | doors of | heaven.

25 He rained down manna also upón them | for to |
eat : ánd | gave them | food from | heaven.

26 So mán did eat | angels' | food : fór he | sent
them | meat e-|nough.

27 He caused the east-wind to blów | under | heaven :
and through his power he bróught | in the | south-
west-|wind.

28  He rained flesh upón them as | thick as | dust :
and feathered fowls líke as the | sand | of the | sea.

29  He let it fáll a-|mong their | tents : even róund
a-|bout their | habit-|ation.

30  So they did eat and were well filled ; for he gáve
them their| own de-|sire : they were nót disap-|pointed |
of their | lust.

31  But while the meat was yet in their mouths, * the
heavy wrath of God came upon them, * and sléw the |
wealthiest | of them : yea and smote down the chosen
mén that | were in | Isra-|el.

32  But for all thís they | sinned yet | more : and
believed | not his | wondrous | works.

33  Therefore their dáys did he con-|sume in |
vanity : ánd their | years | in | trouble.

34  When he sléw them, they | sought | him : and
turned them early, ánd en-|quired | after | God.

35  And they remembered that Gód | was their |
strength : and that the hígh | God was | their red-|
eemer.

36  Nevertheless, they did but flátter him | with
their | mouth : and dissémbled | with him | in their |
tongue.

37  For their héart was not | whole with | him :
neither contínued they | stedfast | in his | covenant.

38  But he was so merciful, that he forgave their
misdeeds, and destróyed | them | not : 39 Yea many
a time turned he his wrath away, * and would not suffer
his whóle dis-|pleasure | to a-|rise.

40  For he considered that they | were but | flesh :
and that they were even a wind that passeth awáy,
and | cometh | not a-|gain.

*Vicissitudes of judgment and faith.*

41 Many a time did they provóke him | in the | wilderness : ánd | grieved him | in the | desert.

42 They turned báck, and | temptcd | God : and moved the Hóly | One in | Isra-|el.

43 They thóught not | of his | hand : and of the day when he delivered them fróm the | hand | of the | enemy;

44 How he had wrought his míracles | in | Egypt : and his wónders | in the | field of | Zoan.


45 He turned their wáters | into | blood : so that they míght not | drink | of the | rivers,

46 He sent lice among them, ánd de-|vourcd them | up : ánd | frogs | to de-|stroy them.

47 He gave their frúit | unto the | caterpillar : ánd their | labour | unto the | grasshopper.

48 He destróyed their | vines with | hailstones : and their múlberry-|trees | with the | frost.

49 He smote their cáttle | also with | hailstones : ánd their | flocks with | hot | thunderbolts.

50 He cast upon them the furiousness of his wrath,* ánger, dis-|pleasure, and | trouble : and sént | evil | angels a-|mong them.

51 He made a way to his indignation, * and spáred not their | soul from | death : but gave their lífe | over | to the | pestilence;

52 And smote áll the | firstborn in | Egypt : the most principal and míghtiest | in the | dwellings of | Ham.

53 But as for his own people, he léd them | forth like | sheep : and carried them ín the | wilderness | like a | flock.

*Retrospect of the divine guidance from Egypt to Canaan.*

54 He brought them out safely, thát they | should not | fear : and overwhélmed their | enemies | with the | sea.

55 And brought them within the bórders | of his | sanctuary : even to his mountain which he púrchased | with his | right | hand.

56 He cast out the héathen | also be-|fore them : caused their land to be divided among them for an heritage, * and made the tribes of Ísrael to | dwell in | their | tents.

57 So they temptcd and displéased the | most high | God : ánd | kept | not his | testimonies ; Apostacy<br>in Canaan

58 But turned their backs, and fell awáy | like their | forefathers : starting asíde | like a | broken | bow.

59 For they grieved him wíth their | hill-|altars : and provoked him tó dis-|pleasure | with their | images.

60 When God heard thís, | he was | wroth : and took sóre dis-|pleasure at | Isra-|el. followed<br>by severer<br>chastise-<br>ments.

61 So that he forsook the tábern-|acle in | Silo : even the tent that hé had | pitched a-|mong | men.

62 He delivered their pówer | into capt-|ivity : and their béauty | into the | enemy's | hand.

63 He gave his people over álso | unto the | sword : ánd was | wroth with | his in-|heritance.

64 The fire consúmed their | young | men : and their maídens | were not | given to | marriage.

65 Their priests were slaín | with the | sword : and there were no wídows to | make | lament-|ation.

66 So the Lord awaked as óne | out of | sleep : and like a | giant re-|freshed with | wine. God's<br>righteous<br>judgment

67 He smote his enemies ín the | hinder | parts :   and abiding kingdom.
and pút them | to a per-|petual | shame.

68 He refused the tábern-|acle of | Joseph : and
chóse | not the | tribe of | Ephraim ;

69 But chóse the | tribe of | Judah : even the híll
of | Sion | which he | loved.

70 And there he búilt his | temple on | high : and
laid the foundation of it like the gróund which | he
hath | made con-|tinually.

71 He chose Dávid | also his | servant : and tóok
him a-|way | from the | sheep-folds.

72 As he was following the éwes great with | young
ones he | took him : that he might feed Jacob his
péople, * and | Israel | his in-|heritance.

73 So he fed them with a fáithful and | true | heart :
and ruled them prúdent-|ly with | all his | power.


### Morning Prayer.

### PSALM LXXIX.   *Deus, venerunt.*

O GOD, the heathen are cóme into | thine in-|   The deso-
heritance : thy holy temple have they defiled, *   lation of
Jerusalem.
and made Jerúsa-|lem an | heap of | stones.

2 The dead bodies of thy servants have they given
to be meat unto the fówls | of the | air : and the flesh
of thy saints únto the | beasts | of the | land.

3 Their blood have they shed like water on every
síde | of Je-|rusalem : ánd there was | no man to |
bury | them.

4 We are become an open sháme | to our | enemies :
a very scorn and derision unto thém | that are | round
a-|bout us.

5 Lord, how lóng wilt | thou be | angry : shall thy
jéalousy | burn like | fire for | ever?

6 Pour out thine indignation upon the héathen that |
have not | known thee : and upon the kingdoms that
háve not | called up-|on thy | Name.

7 For théy have de-|voured | Jacob : and láid |
waste his | dwelling-|place.

8 O remember not our old sins, * but have mercy
upón us, and | that | soon : fór we are | come to |
great | misery.

9 Help us O God of our salvation, * for the glóry |
of thy | Name : O deliver us, and be merciful unto
our síns, * | for thy | Name's | sake.

10 Whérefore do the | heathen | say :"Whére | is |
now their | God?"

11 O let the vengeance of thy servants' blóod | that
is | shed : be openly shewed upón the | heathen | in
our | sight.

12 O let the sorrowful sighing of the prísoners |
come be-|fore thee : according to the greatness of
thy power, preserve thou thóse that | are ap-|pointed
to | die.

13 And for the blasphemy wherewith our neighbours
háve blas-|phemed | thee : reward thou them O Lórd, |
seven-fold | into their | bosom.

14 So we that are thy people and sheep of thy
pasture, * shall gíve thee | thanks for | ever : and will
alway be shewing forth thy praise from géner-|ation to |
gener-|ation.

## PSALM LXXX. *Qui regis Israel.*

HEAR O thou Shepherd of Israel, * thou that Invocation of the God of Israel, leadest Jóseph | like a | sheep : shew thyself also, thóu that | sittest up-|on the | cherubims.

2 Before Ephraim, Bénjamin, | and Ma-|nasses : stír up thy | strength, * and | come, and | help us.

3 *Túrn us a-|gain, O | God : shew the light of thy cóuntenance, | and we | shall be | whole.*

4 O Lórd | God of | hosts : how long wilt thou be in sore distress. ángry | with thy | people that | prayeth ?

5 Thou feedest them with the | bread of | tears : and givest them plénteous-|ness of | tears to | drink.

6 Thou hast made us a very strífe | unto our | neighbours : and our énemies | laugh | us to | scorn.

7 *Turn us agaín, thou | God of | hosts : shew the light of thy cóuntenance, | and we | shall be | whole.*

8 Thou hast brought a víne | out of | Egypt : thou The history of Israel in a figure. hast cast óut the | heathen, and | planted | it.

9 Thou mádest | room for | it : and when it had táken | root it | filled the | land.

10 The hills were covered wíth the | shadow | of it : and the boughs thereóf were | like the | goodly | cedar-trees.

11 She stretched out her bránches | unto the | sea : ánd her | boughs | unto the | river.

12 Why hast thou then bróken | down her | hedge : that all théy that go | by pluck | off her | grapes ?

13 The wild boar out of the woód doth | root it | up : and the wild béasts | of the | field de-|vour it.

14 Turn thee again thou God of hosts, * lóok | down from | heaven : bé-|hold, and | visit this | vine ;

15 And the place of the vineyard that thý right | hand hath | planted : and the branch that thou mádest so | strong | for thy-|self.

16 It is burnt with fíre, and | cut | down : and they shall perish át the re-|buke | of thy | countenance.

17 Let thine hand be upon the mán of | thy right | hand : and upon the son of man, whom thou mádest so | strong for | thine own | self.

18 And so will not wé go | back from | thee : O let us live, and wé shall | call up-|on thy | Name.

19 *Turn us again, O Lórd | God of | hosts : shew the light of thy coúntenance, | and we | shall be | whole.*

## PSALM LXXXI. *Exultate Deo.*

SING we merrily únto | God our | strength : make a cheerful noíse | unto the | God of | Jacob.    *A call to keep festival.*

2 Take the psálm, bring | hither the | tabret : the mérry | harp | with the | lute.

3 Blow up the trúmpet in the | new-|moon : even in the time appointed, ánd up-|on our | solemn | feast-day.

4 For this was made a státute for | Isra-|el : and a láw | of the | God of | Jacob.

5 This he ordained in Jóseph | for a | testimony : when he came out of the land of Egypt, * ánd had | heard a | strange | language.

6 "I eased his shóulder | from the | burden : and his hánds were de-|livered from | making the | pots.    *God's pleading with His people.*

7 "Thou calledst upon me in troubles, and Í de-| His disci-
livered | thee : and heard thee what tíme as the |   pline.
storm | fell up-|on thee.

8 "I | proved thee | also : át the | waters | of |
strife.

9 "Hear O my people, and I will assúre thee, O |  His cove-
Isra-|el : if thou wilt | hearken | unto | me,           nant.

10 "There shall no strange gód | be in | thee :
neither shalt thou wórship | any | other | god.

11 "I am the Lord thy God, * who brought thee oút
of the | land of | Egypt : open thy móuth | wide, and|
I shall | fill it.

12 "But my people wóuld not | hear my | voice : The
and Ísrael | would | not o-|bey me.                    people's
                                                        disobe-
13 "So I gave them up únto their | own hearts' |  dience
lusts : and let them fóllow their | own im-|agin-|
ations.

14 "O that my people would have heárkened | unto |  contrasted
me : for if Ísrael had | walked | in my | ways,         with God's
                                                        purpose.
15 "I should sóon have put | down their | enemies :
and túrned my | hand a-|gainst their | adversaries.

16 "The haters of the Lord shóuld have been |
found | liars : but théir time | should·have en-|dured
for | ever.

17 "He should have fed them álso with the | finest |
wheat-flour : and with honey out of the stony róck
should | I have | satisfied | thee."

Ebening Prayer.

## PSALM LXXXII. *Deus stetit.*

G OD standeth in the cóngreg-|ation of | princes : The com-
hé is a | Judge a-|mong | gods. ing of God
to judg-
ment.

2 "How long will ye gíve | wrong | judgement : and His sen-
accépt the | persons | of the un-|godly? tence.

3 "Defénd the | poor and | fatherless : see that
such as are in néed and ne-|cessity | have | right.

4 "Delíver the | out-cast · and | poor : save them
fróm the | hand of | the un-|godly.

5 "They will not be learned nor understand, * but
wálk on | still in | darkness : all the foundátions of
the | earth are | out of | course.

6 "I have sáid, | Ye are | gods : and ye are all the
chíldren | of the | most | Highest.

7 "Bút ye shall | die like | men : ánd | fall like |
one of the | princes."

8 Arise O God, and júdge | thou the | earth : Prayer to
for thou shalt táke all | heathen to | thine in-|herit- God as
Judge.
ánce.

## PSALM LXXXIII. *Deus, quis similis?*

H OLD not thy tongue O God, kéep | not still | The con-
silence : refráin | not thy-|self, O | God. federacy of
the nations
2 For lo, thine énemies | make a | murmuring : and against
they that háte thee have | lift | up their | head. Israel.

3 They have imagined cráftily a-|gainst thy |
people : and taken cóunsel a-|gainst thy | secret |
ones.

4 They have said, Come and let us root them out, that they bé no | more a | people : and that the name of Israel may bé no | more | in re-|membrance.

5 For they have cast their heads togéther with | one con-|sent : and áre con-|feder-|ate a-|gainst thee ;

6 The tabernacles of the Édomites, | and the | Ismaelites : thé | Moab-|ites, and | Hagarens ;

7 Gébal, and | Ammon, and | Amalek : the Phílis-tines, with | them that | dwell at | Tyre.

8 Assur álso is | joined | with them : ánd have | holpen the | children of | Lot.

9 But do thou to thém as | unto the | Madianites : unto Sisera and unto Jábin | at the | brook of | Kison ; *Prayer for their over-throw.*

10 Whó | perished at | Endor : and becáme as the| dung | of the | earth.

11 Make them and their prínces like | Oreb and | Zeb : yea, make all their princes líke as | Zeba | and Sal-|mana ;

12 Who say, Let us táke | to our-|seives : the hóuses of | God | in pos-|session.

13 O my God, make them líke | unto a | wheel : and ás the | stubble be-|fore the | wind ;

14 Like as the fire that búrneth | up the | wood : and as the fláme | that con-| sumeth the | moun-tains.

15 Persecute them even só | with thy | tempest : and máke them a-|fraid | with thy | storm.

16 Make their fáces a-|shamed, O | Lord : thát | they may | seek thy | Name.

17 Let them be confounded and véxed ever | more

and | more : lét them be | put to | shame, and | perish.

18 And they shall know that thou whose Náme | is Je-|hovah : art only the most Híghest | over | all the | earth.


## PSALM LXXXIV. *Quam dilecta!*

O HOW ámiable | are thy | dwellings : thóu | Lord | of | hosts !

2 My soul hath a desire and longing to enter into the córts | of the | Lord : my heart and my flesh rejóice | in the | living | God.

3 Yea the sparrow hath found her an house, * and the swallow a nest whére she may | lay her | young : even thy altars O Lord of hósts, * my | King | and my | God.

4 Blessed are they that dwéll | in thy | house : théy will be | alway | praising | thee.

*Blessed-ness of those whose house is the house of God:*

5 Blessed is the man whose stréngth | is in | thee : ín whose | heart are | thy | ways.

6 Who going through the vale of misery úse it | for a | well : ánd the | pools are | filled with | water.

7 They will gó from | strength to | strength : and unto the God of gods appeareth évery | one of | them in | Sion.

8 O Lord God of hósts, | hear my | prayer : héarken,| O | God of | Jacob.

*who jour-ney Sion-wards.*

9 Behold O Gód | our de-|fender : and look upón the | face of | thine An-|ointed.

*Rest in the Divine Presence.*

10 For óne day in | thy | courts : ís | better | than a | thousand.

11 I had rather be a door-keeper in the hóuse | of my | God : than to dwéll in the | tents | of un-| godliness.

12 For the Lord is a líght | and de-|fence : the Lord will give grace and worship, * and no good thing shall he withhold from thém that | live a | godly| life.

13 O Lórd | God of | hosts : blessed is the mán that | putteth his | trust in | thee.


PSALM LXXXV.    *Benedixisti, Domine.*

LORD, thou art become grácious | unto thy | land :
     thou hast turned awáy the capt-|ivi-|ty of | Jacob.

2 Thou hast forgiven the offénce | of thy | people : ánd | covered | all their | sins.

3 Thou hast taken awáy all | thy dis-|pleasure : and turned thyself fróm thy | wrathful | indig-|nation.

Thanksgiving for restoration from captivity.

4 Turn us thén, O | God our | Saviour : and lét thine | anger | cease | from us.

5 Wilt thou be displéased at | us for | ever : and wilt thou stretch out thy wrath from óne gener-|ation | to an-|other ?

6 Wilt thou not turn agáin, and | quicken | us : that thy péople | may re-|joice in | thee ?

7 Shéw us thy | mercy, O | Lord : ánd | grant us | thy sal-|vation.

The people's prayer for fresh deliverance.

8 I will hearken what the Lord God will sáy con-| cerning | me : for he shall speak peace unto his

The voice of divine promise.

people and to his sáints, * that they | turn | not a-|
gain.

9 For his salvation is nígh | them that | fear him :
that glóry may | dwell | in our | land.

10 Mercy and trúth are | met to-|gether : ríghteous-
ness and | peace have | kissed each | other.

11 Truth shall flóurish | out of the | earth : and
ríghteousness hath | looked | down from | heaven.

12 Yea the Lord shall shéw | loving-|kindness : ánd
our | land shall | give her | increase.

13 Ríghteousness shall | go be-|fore him : and he
shall diréct his | going | in the | way.

### Morning Prayer.

### PSALM LXXXVI. *Inclina, Domine.*

BOW down thine eár, O | Lord, and | hear me :   Prayer for
for Í am | poor, | and in | misery.                help in
                                                   distress,

2 Preserve thou my sóul, for | I am | holy : my
God, save thy sérvant that | putteth his | trust in |
thee.

3 Be merciful únto | me, O | Lord : for Í will |
call | daily up-|on thee.

4 Comfort the sóul | of thy | servant : for unto thee
O Lórd, do I | lift | up my | soul.

5 For thou Lórd, art | good and | gracious : and
of great mercy unto áll | them that | call up-|on thee.

6 Give ear Lórd, | unto my | prayer : and ponder
the voíce | of my | humble de-|sires.

7 In the time of my trouble Í will | call upon |
thee : fór | thou | hearest | me.

8 Among the gods there is none líke unto | thee,
O | Lord : there is not óne that can | do as | thou |
doest.

resting on the con-fession of God's greatness,

9 All nations whom thou hast made * shall come
and wórship | thee, O | Lord : ánd shall | glori-|fy
thy | Name.

10 For thou art great, and dóest | wondrous |
things : thóu | — art | God a-|lone.

11 Teach me thy way O Lord, * and I will wálk | in
thy | truth : O knit my heart unto thée, that | I may |
fear thy | Name.

12 I will thank thee O Lord my Gód, with | all
my | heart : and will práise thy | Name for | ever-|
more.

13 For gréat is thy | mercy | toward me : and
thou hast delivered my sóul | from the | nethermost |
hell.

14 O God, the próud arc | risen a-|gainst me : and
the congregations of naughty men have sought after
my soul, * and have nót set | thee be-|fore their |
eyes.

which is challenged by the un-godly.

15 But thou O Lord God, art fúll of com-|passion
and | mercy : long-súffering, | plenteous in | goodness
and | truth.

16 O turn thee then unto mé and have | mercy up-|
on me : give thy strength unto thy servant, * and hélp
the | son | of thine | handmaid.

17 Shew some token upon me for good, * that they
who hate me may sée it, and | be a-|shamed : because
thou Lord, hast hólpen | me, and | comforted | me.

## PSALM LXXXVII. *Fundamenta ejus.*

HER foundations are upón the | holy | hills : the Lord loveth the gates of Sion * móre than | all the | dwellings of | Jacob.

*The glory of Sion,*

2 Very excellent thíngs are | spoken of | thee : thóu | city | of | God.

3 I will thínk upon | Rahab and | Babylon : with | them that | know | me.

4 Behóld ye the | Philistines | also : and they of Tyre with the Morians ; * *ló,* | *there* | *was he* | *born.*

*which shall number the nations among her citizens,*

5 And of Sion it shall be reported * that hé was | born in | her : ánd the most | High shall | stablish | her.

6 The Lord shall rehearse it when he wríteth | up the | people : *thát* | *he was* | *born* | *there.*

7 The singers also and trúmpeters shall | he re-| hearse : Áll my fresh | springs shall | be in | thee.

*in holy joy.*

## PSALM LXXXVIII. *Domine Deus.*

O LORD God of my salvation, I have cried dáy and | night be-|fore thee : O let my prayer enter into thy presence, inclíne thine | ear | unto my | calling.

*The lament of one who finds no relief or light in affliction.*

2 For my sóul is | full of | trouble : and my lífe draweth | nigh | unto | hell.

3 I am counted as one of them that go dówn | into the | pit : and I have been éven as a | man that | hath no | strength.

4 Free among the dead, * like unto them that are wounded and líe | in the | grave : who are out of remembrance, * and are cút a-|way | from thy| hand.

5 Thou hast láid me in the | lowest | pit : in a pláce of | darkness, and | in the | deep.

6 Thine indignation líeth | hard up-|on me : and thou hast véxed | me with | all thy | storms.

7 Thou hast put away mine acquáintance | far from | me : and máde me to | be ab-|horred | of them.

8 I am só | fast in | prison : thát I | cannot | get | forth.

9 My sight fáileth for | very | trouble : Lord I have called daily upon thee, * I have stretched fórth my | hands | unto | thee.

10 Dost thou shew wónders a-|mong the | dead : or shall the déad rise | up a-|gain, and | praise thee ?

11 Shall thy loving-kindness be shéwed | in the | grave : ór thy | faithfulness | in de-|struction ?

12 Shall thy wondrous works be knówn | in the | dark : and thy righteousness in the lánd where | all things | are for-|gotten ?

13 Unto thée have I | cried, O | Lord : and eárly shall my | prayer | come be-|fore thee.

14 Lord why abhórrest | thou my | soul : and hídest | thou thy | face | from me ?

15 I am in misery, and like unto him that is át the | point to | die : even from my youth up thy terrors have I súffered | with a | troubled | mind.

16 Thy wrathful displeasure góeth | over | me : and the féar of | thee | hath un-|done me.

17 They came round abóut me | daily like | water : and cómpassed me to-|gether on | every | side.

18 My lovers and friends hast thou pút a-|way
from | me : and híd mine ac-|quaintance | out of my |
sight.

### Ebening Prayer.

## PSALM LXXXIX.    *Misericordias Domini.*

**M**Y song shall be alway of the loving-kíndness |   The faith-
of the | Lord : with my mouth will I ever be   fulness of
God.
shewing thy truth from óne gener-|ation | to an-|
other.

2 For I have said, Mercy shall be sét | up for |
ever : thy trúth shalt thou | stablish | in the |
heavens.

3 I have made a cóvenant | with my | chosen : I   His cove-
have swórn | unto | David my | servant ;   nant.

4 Thy séed will I | stablish for | ever : and set up
thy throne from óne gener-|ation | to an-|other.

5 O Lord, the very heavens shall práise thy | won-   The great-
drous | works : and thy truth in the cóngreg-|ation |   ness of God
of the | saints.

6 For who is hé a-|mong the | clouds : thát shall
be com-|pared | unto the | Lord ?

7 And what is hé a-|mong the | gods : thát shall
be | like | unto the | Lord ?

8 God is very greatly to be feared in the cóuncil |
of the | saints : and to be had in reverence of all
thém | that are | round a-|bout him.

9 O Lord God of hosts, who is líke | unto | thee :   as Con-
thy truth most mighty Lórd, | is on | every | side.   queror,
Creator,
Ruler,
10 Thou rulest the ráging | of the | sea : thou
stillest the wáves there-|of when | they a-|rise.

11 Thou hast subdued Egypt, ánd de-|stroyed | it :
thou hast scattered thine enemies abróad | with thy |
mighty | arm.

12 The heavens are thine, the eárth | also is | thine :
thou hast laid the foundation of the round wórld, and |
all that | therein | is.

13 Thou hast made the nórth | and the | south :
Tabor and Hermon sháll re-|joice | in thy | Name.

14 Thóu hast a | mighty | arm : strong is thy hánd,
and | high is | thy right | hand.

15 Righteousness and equity are the habitátion | of
thy | seat : mercy and trúth shall | go be-|fore thy |
face.

16 Blessed is the people O Lord, that cán re-|joice
in | thee : they shall wálk in the | light | of thy |
countenance.

17 Their delight shall be dáily | in thy | Name :
and in thy ríghteousness | shall they | make their |
boast.

18 For thou art the glóry | of their | strength :
and in thy loving-kindness thóu shalt | lift | up our |
horns.

19 For the Lórd is | our de-|fence : the Hóly One
of | Israel | is our | King.

------

20 Thou spakest sometime in visions únto thy | The pro-
saints, and | saidst : "I have laid help upon one that mise to
is mighty; * I have exálted one | chosen | out of the | David
people.

21 "I have fóund | David my | servant : with my
holy oíl have | I an-|ointed | him.

22 "My hánd shall | hold him | fast : ánd my |
arm shall | strengthen | him.

23 "The enemy shall not be áble to | do him |
violence : the són of | wickedness | shall not | hurt
him.

24 "I will smite down his fóes be-|fore his | face :
ánd | plague | them that | hate him.

25 "My truth also and my mércy | shall be | with
him : and in my Náme shall his | horn | be ex-|
alted.

26 "I will set his dominion álso | in the | sea : ánd
his | right hand | in the | floods.

27 "He shall call me, Thóu | art my | Father : my
Gód, | and my | strong sal-|vation.

28 "And I will máke | him my | first-born : hígher
than the | kings | of the | earth.

29 "My mercy will I keep for hím for | ever-|
more : and my cóvenant shall | stand | fast | with
him.

30 "His seed also will I máke to en-|dure for | ever :
and his thróne | as the | days of | heaven.

31 "But if his chíldren for-|sake my | law : ánd | sure even<br>in chastise-<br>ments.
walk not | in my | judgements ;

32 "If they break my statutes, and kéep not | my
com-|mandments : I will visit their offences with the
ród, | and their | sin with | scourges.

33 "Nevertheless, my loving-kindness will I not
útterly | take from | him : nór | suffer my | truth to |
fail.            .

34 "My covenant will I not break, nor alter the
thing that is góne | out of my | lips : I have sworn
once by my holiness, thát I | will not | fail | David.

35 "His séed shall en-|dure for | ever : and his séat
is | like as the | sun be-|fore me.

36 "He shall stand fast for evermóre | as the |
moon : and ás the | faithful | witness in | heaven."

---

37 But thou hast abhorred and forsáken | thine An-|
ointed : ánd | art dis-|pleased | at him.

The appeal of the people, forsaken

38 Thou hast broken the cóvenant | of thy | servant :
and cást his | crown | to the | ground.

39 Thou hast overthrówn | all his | hedges : ánd |
broken | down his | strong holds.

40 All théy that go | by | spoil him : and he is
becóme a re-|proach | to his | neighbours.

41 Thou hast set up the right hánd | of his | ene-
mies : and made all his ádvers-|aries | to re-|joice.

and defeated,

42 Thou hast taken away the édge | of his | sword :
and givest him nót | victory | in the | battle.

43 Thóu hast put | out his | glory : and cást his |
throne | down to the | ground.

44 The days of his yóuth | hast thou | shortened :
ánd | covered him | with dis-|honour.

45 Lord how long wilt thou híde thy-|self, for |
ever : and sháll thy | wrath | burn like | fire ?

in regard of the shortness of the time,

46 O remember how shórt my | time | is : where-
fore hast thou máde | all | men for | nought ?

47 What man is he that líveth, and shall | not see |
death : and shall he deliver his sóul | from the | hand
of | hell ?

48 Lord where are thy óld | loving-|kindnesses :
which thou swárest unto | David | in thy | truth ?

and the promises of God.

49 Remember Lord the rebúke that thy | servants |
have : and how I do bear in my bósom the re-|bukes
of | many | people ;

50 Wherewith thine énemies have | blasphemed |

thee : and slándered the | footsteps of | thine An-|
ointed.

---

*Praised be the Lórd for* | *ever-|more* : *Á-|men, and* |
*A-|men.*

### 𝔐orning 𝔓rayer.

## PSALM XC. *Domine, refugium.*

LORD, thóu hast | been our | refuge : from óne
gener-|ation | to an-|other. Transitori-
ness of
man before
2 Before the mountains were brought forth, * or God.
ever the eárth and the | world were | made : thou art
God from everlásting, and | world with-|out | end.

3 Thou turnest mán | to de-|struction : again thou
sayest, Cóme a-|gain, ye | children of | men.

4 For a thousand years in thý sight * are | but as |
yesterday : seeing that is pást as a | watch | in the |
night.

5 As soon as thou scatterest them they are éven |
as a | sleep : and fáde away | suddenly | like the |
grass.

6 In the morning it is gréen, and | groweth | up :
but in the evening it is cut dówn, | dried | up, and |
withered.

7 For we consume awáy in | thy dis-|pleasure : and
are afraíd at thy | wrathful | indig-|nation.

8 Thou hast sét our mis-|deeds be-|fore thee : and
our secret síns in the | light | of thy | countenance.

9 For when thou art angry áll our | days are |
gone : we bring our years to an end, as it wére a |
tale | that is | told.

10 The days of our age are threescore years and ten ; * and though men be so strong that they cóme to | fourscore | years : yet is their strength then but labour and sorrow ; * so soon pásseth it a-|way, and | we are | gone.

11 But who regardeth the pówer | of thy | wrath : for even thereafter as a man féareth, | so is | thy dis-| pleasure.

12 So teách us to | number our | days : that we may applý our | hearts | unto | wisdom.

13 Turn thee again O Lórd, | at the | last : ánd be | gracious | unto thy | servants. *Prayer for restoration.*

14 O satisfy us with thy mércy, and | that | soon : so shall we rejoice and be glád all the | days | of our | life.

15 Comfort us again now after the time that thóu hast | plagued | us : and for the years whereín | we have | suffered ad-|versity.

16 Shéw thy | servants thy | work : ánd their | children | thy | glory.

17 And the glorious Majesty of the Lord our Gód | be up-|on us : prosper thou the work of our hands upon us, * O prósper | thou our | handy-|work.

## PSALM XCI. *Qui habitat.*

WHOSO dwelleth under the defénce of the | most | High : shall abide únder the | shadow | of the Al-|mighty. *Confession.*

2 I will say unto the Lord, Thou art my hópe, | and my | strong hold : my Gód, in | him | will I | trust.

3 For he shall deliver thee from the snáre | of the | **The divine protection.**
hunter : ánd | from the | noisome | pestilence.

4 He shall defend thee under his wings, * and thou
shalt be sáfe | under his | feathers : his faithfulness
and trúth shall | be thy | shield and | buckler.

5 Thou shalt not be afraíd for any | terror by |
night : nór for the | arrow that | flieth by | day;

6 For the péstilence that | walketh in | darkness :
nor for the síckness that de-|stroyeth | in the | noon-
day.

7 A thousand shall fall beside thee, * and ten thóu-
sand at | thy right | hand : bút it shall | not come |
nigh | thee.

8 Yea with thine éyes shalt | thou be-|hold : and
sée the re-|ward of | the un-|godly.

9 For thou Lórd, | art my | hope : thou hast set **Con-**
thine hóuse of de-|fence | very | high.     **fession.**

10 There shall no evil háppen | unto | thee : nei- **The divine**
ther shall ány | plague come | nigh thy | dwelling.  **protection.**

11 For he shall give his angels chárge | over |
thee : to kéep | thee in | all thy | ways.

12 They shall béar thee | in their | hands : that
thou húrt not thy | foot a-|gainst a | stone.

13 Thou shalt go upón the | lion and | adder : the
young lion and the dragon shált thou | tread | under
thy | feet.

14 " Because he hath set his love upon me, therefore **The divine**
will Í de-|liver | him : I will set him up, becaúse | he  **voice.**
hath | known my | Name.

15 " He shall cáll upon me and | I will | hear him :

yea I am with him in trouble; * I will delíver him, and | bring | him to | honour.

16 "With long life will I | satisfy | him **:** ánd | shew him | my sal-|vation."

## PSALM XCII. *Bonum est confiteri.*

I T is a good thing to give thánks | unto the | Lord **:** *The joy of thanks-giving.*
and to sing praises únto thy | Name, | O most |
Highest;

2 To tell of thy loving-kindness éarly | in the | morning **:** and of thy trúth | in the | night-|season;

3 Upon an instrument of ten strings, ánd up-|on the | lute **:** upon a loud ínstrument, | and up-|on the | harp.

4 For thou Lord, hast made me gláth | through thy | works **:** and I will rejoice in giving praise for the óper-|ations | of thy | hands.

5 O Lord how glórious | are thy | works **:** thý | thoughts are | very | deep.

6 An unwise man doth not wéll con-|sider | this **:** and a fóol | doth not | under-|stand it.

7 When the ungodly are green as the grass, * and *The pros-perity of the wicked,*
when all the workers of wícked-|ness do | flourish **:** thén shall | they · be de-|stroyed for | ever.

But thou Lórd | art the · most | Highest **:** fór |—| ever-|more.

8 For lo thine enemies O Lord, * lo thine énem-|ies shall | perish **:** and all the workers of wícked-|ness shall | be de-|stroyed.

9 But mine horn shall be exalted like the hórn | of *and of the righteous.*
an | unicorn **:** for I am an-|ointed with | fresh | oil.

20

10 Mine eye also shall see his lúst | of mine | ene-
mies : and mine ear shall hear his desire of the wícked
that a-|rise | up a-|gainst me.

11 The righteous shall flóurish | like a | palm-tree :
and shall spread abróad | like a | cedar in | Libanus.

12 Such as are planted in the hoúse | of the | Lord :
shall flourish in the cóurts of the | house | of our |
God.

13 They also shall bring forth more frúit | in their |
age : ánd shall be | fat and | well-|liking.

14 That they may shew how true the Lórd my |
strength | is : and that there is nó un-|righteous-|ness
in | him.

### Ebening Prayer.

### PSALM XCIII. *Dominus regnavit.*

THE Lord is King, and hath put on glóri-|ous The
ap-|parel : the Lord hath put on his appárel God in
and | girded him-|self with | strength. creation,

The majesty of God in creation,

2 He hath made the róund | world so | sure : thát
it | cannot | be | moved.

3 Ever since the world began hath thy séat | been
pre-|pared : thóu | art from | ever-|lasting.

4 The floods are risen O Lord, * the floods have in sove-
líft | up their | voice : thé | floods lift | up their | reignty,
waves.

5 The waves of the sea are míghty * and | rage |
horribly : but yet the Lórd, who | dwelleth on | high,
is | mightier.

6 Thy testimonies O Lórd, are | very | sure : hóli- in revela-
ness be-|cometh thine | house for | ever. tion.

## PSALM XCIV. *Deus ultionum.*

O LORD God, to whóm | vengeance be-|longeth : An appeal to God.
thou God to whom véngeance be-|longeth,|
shew thy-|self.

2 Arise thou Júdge | of the | world : and reward
the próud | after | their de-|serving.

3 Lord how lóng | shall · the un-|godly : how lóng | The wicked triumph,
shall · the un-|godly | triumph ?
4 How long shall all wicked doers spéak | so dis-| yet
dainfully : ánd | make such | proud | boasting ?
5 They smite dówn thy | people, O | Lord : ánd |
trouble | thine | heritage.
6 They murder the wídow, | and the | stranger :
and pút the | father-|less to | death.
7 And yet they say Tush, the Lórd | shall not |
see : neither sháll the | God of | Jacob re-|gard it.

8 Take heed ye unwíse a-|mong the | people : O God marks them.
ye fóols when | will ye | under-|stand ?
9 He that planted the eár, shall | he not | hear : or
he that máde the | eye, shall | he not | see ?
10 Or he that núrtur-|eth the | heathen : it is
he that teacheth man knówledge, | shall not | he |
punish ?
11 The Lord knóweth the | thoughts of | man :
thát | they | are but | vain.

12 Blessed is the man whom thou chástenest | O | God's chastise-ments are
Lord : ánd | teachest him | in thy | law ;
13 That thou mayest give him patience ín time | fruitful at last :

20—2

of ad-|versity : until the pit be digged | up for | the
un-|godly.

14 For the Lórd will not | fail his | people : neither
will he for-|sake | his in-|heritance;

15 Until righteousness turn agaín | unto | judge-
ment : all such as are trúe in | heart shall | fol-
low | it.

16 Who will rise up with mé a-|gainst the | wicked : nor does
or who will take my párt a-|gainst the | evil-|doers ? fail;

His help

17 If the Lórd had not | helped | me : it had not
failed but my sóul | had been | put to | silence.

18 But when I saíd, My | foot hath | slipt : thy
mércy O | Lord, | held me | up.

19 In the multitude of the sorrows that I hád | in
my | heart : thy cómforts | have re-|freshed my | soul.

20 Wilt thou have any thing to dó with the | stool and the
of | wickedness : which imágineth | mischief | as a | shall
law ?

wicked

perish.

21 They gather them together against the sóul |
of the | righteous : ánd con-|demn the | innocent |
blood.

22 But the Lórd | is my | refuge : and my Gód is
the | strength | of my | confidence.

23 He shall recompense them their wickedness,*
and destroy them ín their | own | malice : yea the
Lórd our | God | shall de-|stroy them.

### Morning Prayer.

### PSALM XCV. *Venite, exultemus.*

O COME let us síng | unto the | Lord : let us A call to
heartily rejóice in the | strength of | our sal-|
vation.

worship.

2 Let us come before his présence with | thanks-|
giving : and shéw ourselves | glad in | him with |
psalms.

3 For the Lórd is a | great | God : and a gréat |  The great-
ness of
King a-|bove all | gods.  God.

4 In his hand are all the córners | of the | earth :
and the stréngth of the | hills is | his | also.

5 The séa is his, | and he | made it : and his hánds
pre-|pared the | dry | land.

6 O come let us wórship and | fall | down : and  A renewed
call.
knéel be-|fore the | Lord our | Maker.

7 For hé is the | Lord our | God : and we are the
people of his pasture, ánd the | sheep | of his | hand.

8 To-day if ye will hear his voice, * hárden | not  Warnings
against
your | hearts : as in the provocation, * and as in the  neglect.
dáy of tempt-|ation | in the | wilderness ;

9 When your fáthers | tempted | me : próved | me,
and | saw my | works.

10 Forty years long was I grieved with thís gener-|
ation, and | said : It is a people that do err in their
hearts, * fór they | have not | known my | ways ;

11 Unto whom I swáre | in my | wrath : that they
shóuld not | enter | into my | rest.


PSALM XCVI. *Cantate Domino.*

O SING unto the Lórd a | new | song : sing unto  Universal
call to
the Lórd, | all the | whole | earth.  praise
God,
2 Sing unto the Lórd, and | praise his | Name : be
telling of his sal-|vation from | day to | day.

3 Declare his hónour | unto the | heathen : and his wónders | unto | all | people.

4 For the Lord is great, and cannot wórthi-|ly be | praised : he is móre to be | feared than | all | gods. *for His supreme glory.*

5 As for all the gods of the heathen, théy | are but | idols : but it ís the | Lord that | made the | heavens.

6 Glory and wórship | are be-|fore him : pówer and | honour are | in his | sanctuary.

7 Ascribe unto the Lord, O ye kíndreds | of the | people : ascríbe unto the | Lord | worship and | power. *The heathen*

8 Ascribe unto the Lord the honour dúe | unto his | Name : bring présents and | come | into his | courts.

9 O worship the Lórd in the | beauty of | holiness : let the whole eárth | stand in | awe of | him.

10 Tell it out among the héathen that the | Lord is | King : and that it is he who hath made the round world so fast that it cannot be moved ; * and how that hé shall | judge the | people | righteously. *and nature rejoice in Him,*

11 Let the heavens rejoice, and lét the | earth be | glad : let the sea make a nóise, and | all that | therein | is.

12 Let the field be jóyful, and | all · that is | in it : then shall all the trees of the wóod re-|joice be-|fore the | Lord.

13 For he cometh, * for he cómeth to | judge the | earth : and with righteousness to judge the wórld, * and the | people | with his | truth. *the coming Judge.*

## PSALM XCVII. *Dominus regnavit.*

THE Lord is King, the eárth may be | glad
there-|of : yea the multitude of the ísles | may
be | glad there-|of.

2 Clouds and dárkness are | round a-|bout him :
righteousness and judgement are the hábit-|ation | of
his | seat.

3 There shall gó a | fire be-|fore him : and burn up
his énem-|ies on | every | side.

*The sovereignty of God.*

4 His lightnings gave shíne | unto the | world : the
eárth | saw it, and | was a-|fraid.

5 The hills melted like wax at the présence | of
the | Lord : at the presence of the Lórd | of the |
whole | earth.

6 The héavens have de-|clared his | righteousness :
and áll the | people have | seen his | glory.

*The signs of His presence.*

7 Confounded be all they that worship carved
images, * and that delíght in | vain | gods : wórship |
him, | all ye | gods.

8 Sion héard of it, | and re-|joiced : and the
daughters of Judah were glad, * becáuse of thy |
judgements, | O | Lord.

9 For thou Lord art higher than áll that are | in
the | earth : thou art exálted | far a-|bove all | gods.

*His judgments.*

10 O ye that love the Lord, see that ye hate the
thíng | which is | evil : the Lord preserveth the souls
of his saints; * he shall deliver them fróm the | hand
of | the un-|godly.

11 There is sprung up a líght | for the | righteous :
and joyful gládness for | such as | are true-|hearted.

*His subjects.*

12 Rejoice in the | Lord ye | righteous : and give thánks for a re-|membrance | of his | holiness.


### Ebening Prayer.

## PSALM XCVIII. *Cantate Domino.*

O SING unto the Lord a new song, * for he hath dóne | marvellous | things : 2 With his own right hand, and with his holy arm, háth he | gotten him-|self the | victory.  God's victory for His people.

3 The Lord declared | his sal-|vation : his right-eousness hath he openly shéwed in the | sight | of the | heathen.

4 He hath remembered his mercy and truth * toward the hóuse of | Isra-|el : and all the ends of the world * have séen the sal-|vation | of our | God.


5 Shew yourselves joyful unto the Lórd, | all ye | lands : síng, re-|joice, and | give | thanks.  Let men and

6 Praise the Lórd up-|on the | harp : sing to the hárp with a | psalm of | thanks-|giving.

7 With trúmpets | also and | shawms : O shew yourselves jóyful be-|fore the | Lord the | King.


8 Let the sea make a noise, and áll that | therein | is : the round wórld, and | they that | dwell there-|in.  nature praise Him for His judg-ment.

9 Let the floods clap their hands, * and let the hills be joyful togéther be-|fore the | Lord : fór he is | come to | judge the | earth.

10 With righteousness shall he | judge the | world : and the | people | with | equity.

## PSALM XCIX. *Dominus regnavit.*

THE Lord is King, be the people néver | so im-| The Lord is King.
patient : he sitteth between the cherubims, be
the eárth | never | so un-|quiet.

2 The Lórd is | great in | Sion : ánd | high a-|bove
all | people.

3 They shall give thánks | unto thy | Name : which
is gréat, | wonder-|ful, and | holy.

4 The King's power loveth judgement ; * thóu hast
pre-|pared | equity : thou hast executed júdgement
and | righteous-|ness in | Jacob.

5 *O mágnify the | Lord our | God : and fall down
before his fóotstool,* | for | he is | holy.*

6 Moses and Aaron among his priests, * and The witness of history.
Samuel among such as cáll up-|on his | Name : these
called upón the | Lord, | and he | heard them.

7 He spake unto them oút of the | cloudy | pillar :
for they kept his testimonies, * ánd the | law | that he |
gave them.

8 Thou héardest them O | Lord our | God : thou
forgavest them O God, and púnish-|edst their | own
in-|ventions.

9 *O magnify the Lord our God, * and worship him
upón his | holy | hill : fór the | Lord our | God is |
holy.*

## PSALM C. *Jubilate Deo.*

O BE joyful in the Lórd, | all ye | lands : serve A twofold call and ground for worship.
the Lord with gladness, * and come befóre his |
presence | with a | song.

2 Be ye sure that the Lórd | he is | God : it is he

21

that hath made us and not we ourselves ; * we are his people, ánd the | sheep | of his | pasture.

3 O go your way into his gates with thanksgiving, *  ·
and ínto his | courts with | praise : be thankful unto him, and spéak | good | of his | Name.

4 For the Lord is gracious, * his mércy is | ever-|
lasting : and his truth endureth from géner-|ation to | gener-|ation.

PSALM CI. *Misericordiam et judicium.*

M Y sóng shall be of | mercy and | judgement :   The pro-
unto thée, O | Lord, | will I | sing.   fession of
a righteous
2 O lét me have | under-|standing : ín the | way   ruler.
of | godli-|ness.

3 When wilt thou cóme | unto | me : I will walk in my hóuse | with a | perfect | heart.

4 I will take no wicked thing in hand ; * I hate the síns | of un-|faithfulness : there shall nó such | cleave |
unto | me.

5 A froward héart shall de-|part from | me : I wíll not | know a | wicked | person.

6   Whoso privily slánder-|eth his | neighbour :
hím | — will | I de-|stroy.

7 Whoso hath also a proud lóok and | high | stom-ach : Í | will not | suffer | him.

8 Mine eyes look upon such as are faithful | in the |
land : thát | they may | dwell with | me.

9 Whoso léadeth a | godly | life : hé | — shall | be my | servant.

10 There shall no deceitful person dwéll | in my |
house : he that telleth líes shall not | tarry | in my |
sight.

11 I shall soon destroy all the ungódly that are | in the | land : that I may root out all wicked doers fróm the | city | of the | Lord.

### 𝕸orning 𝕻rayer.

### PSALM CII. *Domine, exaudi.*

HÉAR my | prayer O | Lord : and let my crý-ing | come | unto | thee.

Prayer in deep distress.

2 Hide not thy face from me in the tíme | of my | trouble : incline thine ear unto me when I cáll; * O | hear · me and | that right | soon.

3 For my days are consúmed a-|way like | smoke : and my bones are búrnt up | as it | were a | fire-brand.

4 My heart is smitten dówn, and | withered like | grass : so that Í for-|get to | eat my | bread.

5 For the vóice | of my | groaning : my bones will scárce | cleave | to my | flesh.

6 I am become like a pélican | in the | wilderness : and like an ówl | that is | in the | desert.

7 I have watched, and am éven as it | were a | sparrow : that sítteth a-|lone up-|on the | house-top.

8 Mine enemies revíle me | all · the day | long : and they that are mad upón me are | sworn to-|gether a-|gainst me.

9 For I have eaten áshes | as · it were | bread : ánd | mingled my | drink with | weeping;

10 And that because of thine índig-|nation and | wrath : for thou hast táken me | up, and | cast me | down.

11 My days are góne | like a | shadow : and Í am | withered | like | grass.

12 But thou O Lórd shalt en-|dure for | ever : and thy remémbrance through-|out all | gener-|ations.

13 Thou shalt arise and have mércy up-|on | Sion : for it is time that thou have mercy upón her, | yea the | time is | come.

14 And why? thy servants thínk up-|on her | stones : and it pitieth thém to | see her | in the | dust.

15 The heathen shall féar thy | Name O | Lord : and all the kíngs | of the | earth thy | Majesty ;

16 When the Lórd shall | build up | Sion : and whén his | glory | shall ap-|pear ;

17 When he turneth him unto the práyer of the | poor | destitute : ánd de-|spiseth not | their de-|sire.

18 This shall be written for thóse that | come | after : and the people which sháll be | born shall | praise the | Lord.

19 For he hath looked dówn | from his | sanctuary : out of the héaven did the | Lord be-|hold the | earth ;

20 That he might hear the mournings of súch as are | in capt-|ivity : and deliver the chíldren ap-| pointed | unto | death ;

21 That they may declare the Náme of the | Lord in | Sion : ánd his | worship | at Je-|rusalem ;

22 When the péople are | gathered to-|gether : and the kíngdoms | also to | serve the | Lord.

23 He brought down my stréngth | in my | jour-ney : ánd | shortened | my | days.

*Trust in the un-changing mercy of God.*

*The Lord abides for ever, and*

24 But I said, O my God take me not away in the they that
mídst | of mine | age : as for thy years, they endúre abide with
through-|out all | gener-|ations.

25 Thou Lord in the beginning hast laid the foundá-
tion | of the | earth : and the héavens are the | work
of | thy | hands.

26 They shall perish, but thóu | shalt en-|dure :
they áll shall wax | old as | doth a | garment ;

27 And as a vesture shalt thou change them, ánd
they | shall be | changed : but thou art the sáme *
and | thy years | shall not | fail.

28 The children of thy sérvants | shall con-|tinue :
and their seed shall stánd | fast | in thy | sight.

## PSALM CIII. *Benedic, anima mea.*

PRAISE the Lórd, | O my | soul : and all that is   Praise the
within me | praise his | holy | Name.   Lord.

2 Praise the Lórd, | O my | soul : ánd for-|get not |
all his | benefits ;

3 Who forgíveth | all thy | sin : and héaleth | all |
thine in-|firmities ;

4 Who saveth thy lífe | from de-|struction : and
crówneth thee with | mercy and | loving-|kindness ;

5 Who satisfieth thy móuth with | good | things :
making thee yóung and | lusty | as an | eagle.

6 The Lord executeth ríghteous-|ness and | judge-   His
ment : for all thém that | are op-|pressed with |   righteous-
wrong.   ness and
mercy.

7 He shewed his wáys | unto | Moses : his works
únto the | children of | Isra-|el.

8 The Lord is fúll of com-|passion and | mercy :
long-súffering, | and of | great | goodness.

9 He will not | alway be | chiding : neither kéep-eth | he his | anger for | ever.

10 He hath not déalt with us | after our | sins : nor rewárded us ac-|cording | to our | wickednesses.

11 For look how high the heaven is in compárison | of the | earth : so great is his mercy álso | toward | them that | fear him.

12 Look how wide also the éast is | from the | west : so fár hath he | set our | sins from | us.

13 Yea, like as a father pítieth his | own | children : even so is the Lord mérciful | unto | them that | fear him.

14 For he knoweth whereóf | we are | made : he remémbereth | that we | are but | dust.

15 The days of mán are | but as | grass : for he flourisheth ás a | flower | of the | field.

16 For as soon as the wind goeth óver it, | it is | gone : and the place thereóf shall | know it | no | more.

17 But the merciful goodness of the Lord endureth for ever and ever upón | them that | fear him : and his righteousness up-|on | children's | children ;

18 Even upon súch as | keep his | covenant : and think upon | his com-|mandments to | do them.

19 The Lord hath· prepáred his | seat in | heaven : and his kíngdom | ruleth | over | all.

20 O praise the Lord ye angels of his, yé that ex-|cel in | strength : ye that fulfil his commandment, * and hearken únto the | voice | of his | words. *Praise the Lord.*

21 O praise the Lórd, all | ye his | hosts : ye sérvants of | his that | do his | pleasure.

22 O speak good of the Lord all ye works of his, in all pláces of | his dom-|inion : práise thou the | Lord, | O my | soul.

### Ebening Prayer.

### PSALM CIV. *Benedic, anima mea.*

PRAISE the Lórd, | O my | soul : O Lord my God thou art become exceeding glorious ; * thou art clóthed with | majes-|ty and | honour.

The majesty of God in nature.

2 Thou deckest thyself with light as it wére | with a | garment : and spreadest oút the | heavens | like a | curtain.

3 Who layeth the beams of his chámbers | in the | waters : and maketh the clouds his chariot, * and walketh upón the | wings | of the | wind.

4 He máketh his | angels | spirits : and his mínis-| ters a | flaming | fire.

5 He laid the foundátions | of the | earth : that it néver should | move at | any | time.

His creative power in land and water.

6 Thou coveredst it with the deep líke as | with a | garment : the wáters | stand | in the | hills.

7 At thý re-|buke they | flee : at the vóice of thy | thunder they | are a-|fraid.

8 They go up as high as the hills, and dówn to the | valleys be-|neath : even unto the place which thóu | hast ap-|pointed | for them.

9 Thou hast set them their bóunds which they | shall not | pass : neither túrn a-|gain to | cover the | earth.

10 He sendeth the spríngs | into the | rivers : which | run a-|mong the | hills.

11 All beasts of the field | drink there-|of : and the
wild | asses | quench their | thirst.

His provision for living things.

12 Beside them shall the fowls of the áir have
their | habit-|ation : ánd | sing a-|mong the | branches.

13 He watereth the hills | from a-|bove : the earth
is filled with the | fruit | of thy | works.

14 He bringeth forth gráss | for the | cattle : and
green hérb | for the | service of | men ;

15 That he may bring food out of the earth, * and
wine that maketh glád the | heart of | man : and oil
to make him a cheerful countenance, * and bréad to |
strengthen | man's | heart.

16 The trees of the Lord álso are | full of | sap :
even the cedars of Líba-|nus which | he hath |
planted ;

17 Wherein the birds | make their | nests : and the
fir-trees áre a | dwelling | for the | stork.

18 The high hills are a refuge fór the | wild |
goats : and so are the stóny | rocks | for the | conies.

19 He appointed the móon for | certain | seasons :
and the sún | knoweth his | going | down.

The ministry of day and night.

20 Thou makest dárkness that it | may be | night :
wherein all the beásts | of the | forest do | move.

21 The lions roáring | after their | prey : dó | seek
their | meat from | God.

22 The sun ariseth, and they gét them a-|way to-|
gether : and láy them | down | in their | dens.

23 Man goeth forth to his wórk, and | to his |
labour : ún-|——| til the | evening.

24 O Lord how mánifold | are thy | works : in wis-
dom hast thou made them all ; * the eárth is | full | of
thy | riches.

His enduring and triumphant Majesty.

25 So is the gréat and | wide sea | also : wherein are things creeping innumerable, * bóth | small and | great | beasts.

26 There go the ships, and thére is | that Lev-|ia-than : whom thou hast máde to | take his | pastime there-|in.

27 These wáit | all upon | thee : that thou mayest gíve them | meat in | due | season.

28 When thou givest it thém they | gather | it : and when thou openest thy hánd | they are | filled with | good.

29 When thou hidest thy fáce | they are | troubled : when thou takest away their breath they die, * and are túrned a-|gain | to their | dust.

30 When thou lettest thy breath go fórth they | shall be | made : and thou shalt renéw the | face | of the | earth.

31 The glorious Majesty of the Lórd shall en-|dure for | ever : the Lórd shall re-|joice | in his | works. *Confession of His sovereignty.*

32 The earth shall trémble at the | look of | him : if he do but toúch the | hills, | they shall | smoke.

33 I will sing unto the Lórd as | long · as I | live : I will praise my Gód | while I | have my | being.

34 And só shall my | words | please him : my jóy shall | be | in the | Lord.

35 As for sinners, they shall be consumed out of the earth, * and the ungódly shall | come · to an | end : praise thou the Lord O my soúl, * | praise | — the | Lord.

## PSALM CV. *Confitemini Domino.*

O GIVE thanks unto the Lord, and cáll up-|on his | Name : tell the péople what | things | he hath | done.

The good-ness of God to His people.

2 O let your sóngs be of | him, and | praise him : and let your talking bé of | all his | wondrous | works.

3 Rejoíce in his | holy | Name : let the heart of thém re-|joice that | seek the | Lord.

4 Seek the Lórd | and his | strength : séek his | face | ever-|more.

5 Remember the marvellous wórks that | he hath | done : his wonders ánd the | judgements | of his | mouth,

6 O ye seed of Ábra-|ham his | servant : yé | children of | Jacob his | chosen.

7 Hé is the | Lord our | God : his júdgements | are in | all the | world.

His covenant with the fathers.

8 He hath been alway mindful of his cóven-|ant and | promise : that he máde to a | thousand | gener-| ations;

9 Even the covenant thát he | made with | Abra-ham : and the óath that he | sware | unto | Isaac;

10 And appointed the same unto Jácob | for a | law : and to Israel fór an | ever-|lasting | testament;

11 Saying,"Unto thee will I gíve the | land of | Canaan : thé | lot of | your in-|heritance ;"

12 When there were yét but a | few of | them : and théy | strangers | in the | land;

13 What time as they went from one nátion | to an-|other : from one kíngdom | to an-|other | people;

14 He suffered nó man to | do them | wrong : but reproved éven | kings for | their | sakes ;

15 "Tóuch not | mine An-|ointed : ánd | do my | prophets no | harm."

16 Moreover he called for a déarth up-|on the | land : and destróyed | all · the pro-|vision of | bread.

17 But he had sént a | man be-|fore them : even Joseph, who was sóld to | be a | bond-|servant ;

18 Whose feet they húrt | in the | stocks : the íron | entered | into his | soul ;

19 Until the time cáme that his | cause was | known : the wórd | of the | Lord | tried him.

20 The king sént and de-|livered | him : the prínce of the | people | let him · go | free.

21 He made him lórd also | of his | house : ánd | ruler of | all his | substance ;

22 That he might inform his prínces | after his | will : ánd | teach his | senators | wisdom.

23 Israel also cáme | into | Egypt : and Jacob was a stránger | in the | land of | Ham.

24 And he incréased his | people ex-|ceedingly : and máde them | stronger | than their | enemies ;

25 Whose heart turned só that they | hated his | people : and déalt un-|truly | with his | servants.

26 Then sént he | Moses his | servant : ánd | Aaron | whom · he had | chosen.

27 And these shéwed his | tokens a-|mong them : and wónders | in the | land of | Ham.

28 He sent dárkness and | it was | dark : and they were nót ob-|edient | unto his | word.

*The deliverance from Egypt in its preparation,*

*its execution in judgment,*

29 He turned their wáters | into | blood : ánd |
slew | their | fish.

30 Their lánd | brought forth | frogs : yea, éven |
in their | kings' | chambers.

31 He spake the word, and there cáme all | manner
of | flies : ánd | lice in | all their | quarters.

32 He gáve them | hail-stones for | rain : and
flámes of | fire | in their | land.

33 He smote their vínes | also and | fig-trees : and
destroyed the trées | that were | in their | coasts.

34 He spake the word and the grasshoppers came,
and cáter-|pillars in-|numerable : and did eat up all
the grass in their land, and devóured the | fruit | of
their | ground.

35 He smote all the fírst-born | in their | land :
éven the | chief of | all their | strength.

36 He brought them forth álso with | silver and |    its consum-
gold : there was not óne feeble | person a-|mong their |    mation.
tribes.

37 Egypt was glád at | their de-|parting : fór they |
were a-|fraid of | them.

38 He spread out a clóud to | be a | covering : and
fire to give líght | in the | night-|season.

39 At their desíre he | brought | quails : and he
fílled them | with the | bread of | heaven.

40 He opened the rock of stone, and the wáters |
flowed | out : so that rivers rán | in the | dry |
places.

41 For why ? he remémbered his | holy | promise :
ánd | Abra-|ham his | servant.

42 And he brought fórth his | people with | joy :
ánd his | chosen | with | gladness ;

43 And gave them the lánds | of the | heathen : and they took the labours óf the | people | in pos-| session ;

44 That théy might | keep his | statutes : ánd ob-|serve | his | laws.

Ebening Prayer.

### PSALM CVI. *Confitemini Domino.*

O GIVE thanks unto the Lórd, for | he is | gra-cious : ánd his | mercy en-|dureth for | ever.   Praise and prayer.

2 Who can express the noble ácts | of the | Lord : ór | shew forth | all his | praise ?

3 Blessed are théy that | alway keep | judgement : ánd | do | righteous-|ness.

4 Remember me O Lord, according to the favour that thou béarest | unto thy | people : O vísit | me with | thy sal-|vation ;

5 That I may see the felícity | of thy | chosen : and rejoice in the gladness of thy people, * ánd give | thanks with | thine in-|heritance.

6 We have sínned | with our | fathers : we have dóne a-|miss, and | dealt | wickedly.   The sins of the people in

7 Our fathers regarded not thy wonders in Egypt, * contrast neither kept they thy great góodness | in re-|mem-   with God's mercies in brance : but were disobedient at the sea, éven | at   Egypt ; the | Red | sea.

8 Nevertheless, he helped them fór his | Name's | sake : that he might máke his | power | to be | known.

9 He rebuked the Red sea also, ánd it was | dried | up : so he led them thróugh the | deep as | through a | wilderness.

10 And he saved them from the ádvers-|ary's | hand : and delivered them fróm the | hand | of the | enemy.

11 As for those that troubled them, the waters óver-|whelmed | them : there wás not | one | of them | left.

12 Then belíeved | they his | words : and sáng | praise | unto | him.


13 But within a whíle they for-|gat his | works : *in the Exodus;*
ánd would | not a-|bide his | counsel.

14 But lust came upón them | in the | wilderness : and they témpted | God | in the | desert.

15 And he gáve them | their de-|sire : and sent léanness with-|al | into their | soul.

16 They angered Moses álso | in the | tents : and Áaron the | saint | of the | Lord.

17 So the earth ópened and | swallowed up | Da-than : and covered the cóngreg-|ation | of Ab-| iram.

18 And the fire was kíndled | in their | company : the fláme | burnt up | the un-|godly.

19 They máde a | calf in | Horeb : ánd | worship-ped the | molten | image.

20 Thús they | turned their | glory : into the simi-litude óf a | calf that | eateth | hay.

21 And they forgát | God their | Saviour : who had dóne so | great | things in | Egypt;

22 Wondrous wórks in the | land of | Ham : and fearful thíngs | by the | Red | sea.

23 So he said he would have destroyed them, * had not Moses his chosen stood befóre him | in the | gap :

to turn away his wrathful indignátion, | lest he | should de-|stroy them.

24 Yea they thought scórn of that | pleasant | land : and gáve no | credence | unto his | word;

25 But múrmured | in their | tents : and hearkened not únto the | voice | of the | Lord.

26 Then lift he úp his | hand a-|gainst them : to óver-|throw them | in the | wilderness;

27 To cast out their séed a-|mong the | nations : ánd to | scatter them | in the | lands.

28 They joined themselves únto | Baal-|peor : and áte the | offerings | of the | dead.

29 Thus they provoked him to ánger with their | own in-|ventions : ánd the | plague was | great a-| mong them.

30 Then stood up Phíne-|es and | prayed : ánd | so the | plague | ceased.

31 And that was counted únto | him for | righteous-ness : among all postéri-|ties for | ever-|more.

32 They angered him also át the | waters of | strife : so that he púnished | Moses | for their | sakes;

33 Becaúse they pro-|voked his | spirit : so that he spáke unad-|visedly | with his | lips.

34 Neither destróyed | they the | heathen : ás the | *in Canaan.* Lord com-|manded | them;

35 But were míngled a-|mong the | heathen : ánd | learned | their | works.

36 Insomuch that they worshipped their idols, * which túrned to their | own de-|cay : yea, they offered their sóns and their | daughters | unto | devils;

37 And shed innocent blood, even the blood of their sóns and | of their | daughters : whom they

offered unto the idols of Canaan ; <sup>*</sup> and the lánd | was de-|filed with | blood.

38 Thus were they stáined with their | own | works : and went a whóring | with their | own in-|ventions.

39 Therefore was the wrath of the Lord kíndled a-|gainst his | people : insomuch that hé ab-|horred his | own in-|heritance. *The Divine chastisements.*

40 And he gave them over into the hánd | of the | heathen : and they that háted them were | lords | over | them.

41 Their énemies op-|pressed | them : ánd | had them | in sub-|jection.

42 Many a time did hé de-|liver | them : but they rebelled against him with their own inventions, * and were bróught | down | in their | wickedness.

43 Nevertheless, when he sáw | their ad-|versity : he | heard | their com-|plaint.

44 He thought upon his covenant and pitied them, according unto the múltitude | of his | mercies : yea, he made all those that led them awáy | captive to | píty | them.

45 Deliver us O Lord our God, <sup>*</sup> and gather us fróm a-|mong the | heathen : that we may give thanks unto thy holy Name, <sup>*</sup> and máke our | boast | of thy | praise.

---

46 *Blessed be the Lord God of Israel* <sup>*</sup> *from ever-lásting and | world without | end : and let áll the | people say | A-|men.*

## Morning Prayer.

### PSALM CVII. *Confitemini Domino.*

O GIVE thanks unto the Lórd, for | he is | gra-
cious : ánd his | mercy en-|dureth for | ever. *Let all give thanks,*

2 Let them give thanks whom the Lórd | hath *exiles and wanderers,*
red-|eemed : and delivered fróm the | hand | of the |
enemy ;

3 And gathered them out of the lands, from the
eást, and | from the | west : fróm the | north, and |
from the | south.

4 They went astray in the wílderness | out of · the |
way : ánd | found no | city to | dwell in ;

5 Húngry | and | thirsty : théir | soul | fainted | in
them.

6 *So they cried unto the Lórd | in their | trouble :
and he delivered | them from | their di-|stress.*

7 He led them fórth by the | right | way : that they
might gó to the | city | where they | dwelt.

8 *O that men would therefore praise the Lórd | for
his | goodness : and declare the wonders that he dóeth |
for the | children of | men !*

9 For he satisfíeth the | empty | soul : and fílleth
the | hungry | soul with | goodness.

10 Such as sit in darkness and ín the | shadow of | *captives and prisoners,*
death : being fast bóund in | miser-|y and | iron ;

11 Because they rebelled against the wórds | of
the | Lord : and lightly regarded the cóunsel | of
the | most | Highest ;

12 He also brought dówn their | heart through |

heaviness : they fell dówn, and | there was | none to | help them.

13 *So when they cried unto the Lórd | in their | trouble : he delívered them | out of | their di-|stress.*

14 For he brought them out of darkness, and oút of the | shadow of | death : ánd | brake their | bonds in | sunder.

15 *O that men would therefore praise the Lórd | for his | goodness : and declare the wonders that he dóeth | for the | children of | men!*

16 For he hath bróken the | gates of | brass : and smítten the | bars of | iron in | sunder.

17 Foolish men are plágued for | their of-|fence : ánd be-|cause | of their | wickedness. *the sick unto death,*

18 Their soul abhórred all | manner of | meat : and they were éven | hard at | death's | door.

19 *So when they cried unto the Lórd | in their | trouble : he delívered them | out of | their di-|stress.*

20 He sent his wórd, and | healed | them : and théy were | saved from | their de-|struction.

21 *O that men would therefore praise the Lórd | for his | goodness : and declare the wonders that he dóeth | for the | children of | men!*

22 That they would offer unto him the sácrifice of | thanks-|giving : and téll | out his | works with | gladness!

23 They that go dówn to the | sea in | ships : and óccupy their | business | in great | waters ; *storm-tossed seafarers.*

24 These men see the wórks | of the | Lord : ánd his | wonders | in the | deep.

25 For at his word the stórmy | wind a-|riseth :
which lífteth | up the | waves there-|of.

26 They are carried up to the heaven, and dówn
again | to the | deep : their soul melteth awáy be-|
cause | of the | trouble.

27 They reel to and fro, and stagger líke a |
drunken | man : ánd are | at their | wits' | end.

28 *So when they cry unto the Lórd | in their | trou-*
*ble : he delívereth them | out of | their di-|stress.*

29 For he máketh the | storm to | cease : só that
the | waves there-|of are | still.

30 Then are they glad, becáuse they | are at | rest :
and so he bringeth them unto the háven | where they |
would | be.

31 *O that men would therefore praise the Lórd | for*
*his | goodness : and declare the wonders that he dócth |*
*for the | children of | men !*

32 That they would exalt him also in the congregá-
tion | of the | people : and práise him in the | seat |
of the | elders !

33 Who turneth the flóods | into a | wilderness :  The Lord
ánd | drieth | up the | water-springs.  rules the
changes
34 A fruitful lánd | maketh he | barren : for the  of life.
wíckedness of | them that | dwell there-|in.

35 Again, he maketh the wílderness a | standing |
water : and wáter-springs | of a | dry | ground.

36 And thére he | setteth the | hungry : that théy
may | build them a | city to | dwell in ;

37 That they may sow their lánd, and | plant |
vineyards : tó | yield them | fruits of | increase.

38 He blesseth them, so that they múlti-|ply ex-|

ceedingly : and suffereth nót their | cattle | to de-|
crease.

39 And again, when they are mínished and |
brought | low : through oppréssion through | any |
plague or | trouble ;

40 Though he suffer them to be évil in-|treated
through | tyrants : and let them wander óut of the |
way | in the | wilderness ;

41 Yet helpeth he the póor | out of | misery : and
maketh him hóuseholds | like a | flock of | sheep.

42 The righteous will consider thís, | and re-|joice : Man's
and the móuth of all | wickedness | shall be | stopped. lesson.

43 Whoso is wíse will | ponder these | things :
and they shall understand the lóving-|kindness | of
the | Lord.

### Ebening Prayer.

### PSALM CVIII. *Paratum cor meum.*
### (lvii. 8—12 ; and lx. 5—12.)

O GOD my heart is réady my | heart is | ready : Thanks-
I will sing and give praise * with the bést | giving for
member | that I | have. deliver-
ance.

2 Awáke thou | lute, and | harp : I mysélf | will
a-|wake right | early.

3 I will give thanks unto thee O Lórd, a-|mong
the | people : I will sing práises unto | thee a-|mong
the | nations.

4 For thy mercy is gréater | than the | heavens :
and thy trúth | reacheth | unto the | clouds.

5 *Set up thyself O Gód, a-|bove the | heavens : and
thy glóry a-|bove | all the | earth.*

6 That thy belóved may | be de-|livered : let thy right hand sáve | them and | hear thou | me.

7 God hath spóken | in his | holiness : I will rejoíce therefore and divide Sichem, * and méte | out the | valley of | Succoth. An ancient song of triumph.

8 Gilead is míne and Ma-|nasses is | mine : Ephraim also ís the | strength | of my | head.

9 Judah is my law-giver, * Móab | is my | washpot : over Edom will I cast out my shoe; * upón Phi-|listia | will I | triumph.

10 Who will lead me ínto the | strong | city : and whó will | bring me | into | Edom? Prayer in present need.

11 Hast not thou forsáken us, | O | God : and wilt not thou O Gód, go | forth | with our | hosts?

12 O hélp us a-|gainst the | enemy : for váin | is the | help of | man.

13 Through Gód we shall | do great | acts : and it is hé that | shall tread | down our | enemies.

## PSALM CIX. *Deus, laudem.*

HOLD not thy tongue O Gód | of my | praise : for the mouth of the ungodly, yea the móuth of the de-|ceitful is | opened up-|on me. The complaint of the persecuted.

2 And they have spoken agáinst me with | false | tongues : they compassed me about also with words of hatred, * and fought agáinst | me with-|out a | cause.

3 For the love that I had unto them, lo they take nów my | contrary | part : bút I | give myself | unto | prayer.

4 Thus have they rewárded me | evil for | good : ánd | hatred for | my good | will.

5 Set thou an ungodly man to be rúler | over | him : and let Sátan | stand at | his right | hand.

The curses of the ungodly.

6 When sentence is given upon him, lét him | be con-|demned : and let his práyer be | turned | into | sin.

7 Lét his | days be | few : and lét an-|other | take his | office.

8 Lét his | children be | fatherless : ánd | — his | wife a | widow.

9 Let his children be vágabonds and | beg their | bread : let them seek it álso | out of | desolate | places.

10 Let the extortioner consúme | all · that he | hath : and lét the | stranger | spoil his | labour.

11 Let there be nó man to | pity | him : nor to have compássion up-|on his | fatherless | children.

12 Let his postérity | be de-|stroyed : and in the next generation lét his | name be | clean put | out.

13 Let the wickedness of his fathers be had in re-membrance in the síght | of the | Lord : and let not the sín of his | mother be | done a-|way.

14 Let them alway bé be-|fore the | Lord : that he may root out the memórial of | them from | off the | earth ;

15 And that, because his mínd was | not · to do | good : but persecuted the poor helpless man, * that he might slay hím that was | vexed | at the | heart.

16 His delight was in cursing, and it shall háppen | unto | him : he loved not blessing, thérefore shall | it be | far from | him.

17 He clothed himself with cursing, líke as | with a | raiment : and it shall come into his bowels like wáter * and like | oil | into · his | bones.

18 Let it be unto him as the clóke that he | hath up-|on him : and as the gírdle that he is | alway | girded with-|al.

19 Let it thus happen from the Lórd | unto mine | enemies : and to those that spéak | evil a-|gainst my | soul.

The reply of the afflicted.

20 But deal thou with me O Lord God, accórding | unto thy | Name : fór | sweet | is thy | mercy.

21 O deliver me, for Í am | helpless and | poor : ánd my | heart is | wounded with-|in me.

22 I go hence like the shádow | that de-|parteth : and am dríven a-|way | as the | grasshopper.

23 My knées are | weak through | fasting : my flesh is dríed | up for | want of | fatness.

24 I became also a repróach | unto | them : they that loóked up-|on me | shaked their | heads.

25 Hélp me O | Lord my | God : O sáve me ac-|cording | to thy | mercy;

26 And they shall know how that thís is | thy | hand : ánd that | thou, | Lord hast | done it.

27 Though they cúrse yet | bless | thou : and let them be confounded that rise up against me; bút | let thy | servant re-|joice.

28 Let mine ádversaries be | clothed with | shame : and let them cover themselves with their ówn con-| fusion | as · with a | cloke.

29 As for me, I will give great thanks unto the Lórd | with my | mouth : and práise | him a-|mong the | multitude;

Trust in the Lord.

30 For he shall stand at the right hánd | of the | poor : to save his sóul | from un-|righteous | judges.

### Morning Prayer.

## PSALM CX. *Dixit Dominus.*

THE Lórd said | unto my | Lord : "Sit thou on my right hand, * until I máke thine | enem-|ies thy | footstool." The Divine King.

2 The Lord shall send the rod of thy pówer | out of | Sion : "be thou ruler, éven in the | midst a-|mong thine | enemies."

3 In the day of thy power shall the people offer thee free-will offerings * with an | holy | worship : the dew of thy birth is óf the | womb | of the | morning. The Divine High Priest.

4 The Lord swáre and will | not re-|pent : "Thou art a Priest for ever * áfter the | order | of Mel-|chi-sedech."

5 The Lórd upon | thy right | hand : shall wound even kíngs in the | day | of his | wrath. The Divine Conqueror.

6 He shall judge among the heathen ; * he shall fill the pláces with the | dead | bodies : and smite in sun-der the héads | over | divers | countries.

7 He shall drink of the bróok | in the | way : there-fore sháll he | lift | up his | head.

## PSALM CXI. *Confitebor tibi.*

I WILL give thanks unto the Lórd with my | whole | heart : secretly among the fáithful and | in the | congreg-|ation. Thanks to God for IIis works.

2 The wórks of the | Lord are | great : sought out
of all thém | that have | pleasure there-|in.

3 His work is worthy to be práised and | had in |
honour : and his ríghteous-|ness en-|dureth for | ever.

4 The merciful and gracious Lord hath so dóne
his | marvellous | works : that they oúght to be | had |
in re-|membrance.

5 He hath given méat unto | them that | fear him : His providence.
he shall éver be | mindful | of his | covenant.

6 He hath shewed his people the pówer | of his |
works : that he may gíve them the | heritage | of the |
heathen.

7 The works of his hánds are | verity and | judg-
ment : áll | his com-|mandments are | true.

8 They stand fást for | ever and | ever : ánd are |
done in | truth and | equity.

9 He sent redémption | unto his | people : he hath His revelation.
commanded his covenant for ever; * hóly and | re-
verend | is his | Name.

10 The fear of the Lórd is the be-|ginning of | wis-
dom : a good understanding have all they that do
thereafter; * the práise of | it en-|dureth for | ever.

### PSALM CXII. *Beatus vir.*

BLESSED is the mán that | feareth the | Lord : The
blessed-
ness of the
righteous
in his
fortunes
and in his
doings.
he hath gréat de-|light in | his com-|mand-
ments.

2 His seed shall be míghty up-|on | earth : the
generátion of the | faithful | shall be | blessed.

3 Riches and plenteousness shall bé | in his | house :
and his ríghteous-|ness en-|dureth for | ever.

24

4 Unto the godly there ariseth up líght | in the | darkness : hé is | merciful | loving and | righteous.

5 A good man is mérci-|ful and | lendeth : and will guíde his | words | with dis-|cretion.

6 For hé shall | never be | moved : and the right-eous shall be hád in | ever-|lasting re-|membrance.

7 He will not be afráid of any | evil | tidings : for his heart standeth fást and be-|lieveth | in the | Lord.

8 His heart is estáblished and | will not | shrink : until he sée his de-|sire up-|on his | enemies.

9 He hath dispersed abroad, and gíven | to the | poor : and his righteousness remaineth for ever ; * his hórn shall | be ex-|alted with | honour.

10 The ungodly shall sée it and | it shall | grieve him : he shall gnash with his teeth and consume away ; * the desíre of the un-|godly | shall | perish.

### PSALM CXIII. *Laudate, pueri.*

PRAISE the | Lord ye | servants : O práise the | Name | of the | Lord.

*Call to the praise of the Lord,*

2 Blessed be the Náme | of the | Lord : from thís time | forth for | ever-|more.

3 The Lórd's | Name is | praised : from the rising up of the sun unto the góing | down | of the | same.

4 The Lord is hígh a-|bove all | heathen : ánd his | glory a-|bove the | heavens.

*majestic in His glory,*

5 Who is like unto the Lord our God, * that háth his | dwelling so | high : and yet humbleth himself to behold the thíngs that | are in | heaven and | earth ?

6 He taketh up the símple | out·of the | dust : and lífteth the | poor | out·of the | mire ;

*loving to the humble.*

7 That he may sét him | with the | princes : even
with the | princes | of his | people.

8 He maketh the barren wóman to | keep | house :
and to bé a | joyful | mother of | children.

### Ebening Prayer.

## PSALM CXIV. *In exitu Israel.*

WHEN Israel cáme | out of | Egypt : and the
house of Jacob fróm a-|mong the | strange |
people,

*The wonders of the Exodus.*

2 Júdah | was his | sanctuary : ánd | Israel | his
dom-|inion.

3 The séa saw | that and | fled : Jórdan | was |
driven | back.

4 The móuntains | skipped like | rams : and the
líttle | hills like | young | sheep.

5 What aileth thee O thou séa, | that thou | fled-
dest : and thou Jórdan that | thou wast | driven |
back ?

6 Ye mountains, thát ye | skipped like | rams : and
ye líttle | hills like | young | sheep ?

7 Tremble thou earth at the présence | of the |
Lord : at the présence | of the | God of | Jacob ;

8 Who turned the hard rock ínto a | standing |
water : and the flínt-stone | into a | springing | well.

## PSALM CXV. *Non nobis, Domine.*

NOT unto us O Lord, not unto us, * but unto
thy Náme | give the | praise : for thy loving
mércy and | for thy | truth's | sake.

*National deliverance.*

24—2

2 Wherefore sháll the | heathen | say : " Where | —
is | now their | God ? "

3 As for oúr God, | he · is in | heaven : he hath  The vanity
done whátso-|ever | pleased | him.  of idols.

4 Their ídols are | silver and | gold : éven the |
work of | men's | hands.

5 Théy have | mouths, and | speak not : éyes |
have | they, and | see not.

6 Théy have | ears, and | hear not : nóses | have |
they, and | smell not.

7 They have hands and handle not; * féet have |
they, and | walk not : néither | speak they | through
their | throat.

8 They that make them are líke | unto | them : and
so are all súch as | put their | trust in | them.

9 But thou house of Israel, trúst thou | in the |  Trust in
Lord : *hé is their | succour | and de-|fence.*  the Lord !

10 Ye house of Aaron, put your trúst | in the |
Lord : *hé is their | helper | and de- | fender.*

11 Ye that fear the Lord, put your trúst | in the |
Lord : *hé is their | helper | and de-|fender.*

12 The Lord hath been mindful of ús, and | he  Confi-
shall | bless us : even he shall bless the house of  dence.
Israel, * hé shall | bless the | house of | Aaron.

13 He shall bless thém that | fear the | Lord :
bóth | small | and | great.

14 The Lord shall increáse you | more and | more :  The
yóu | and | your | children.  Divine
promise.

15 Ye are the bléssed | of the | Lord : whó | made |
heaven and | earth.

16 All the whole heávens | are the | Lord's : the Praise.
earth hath he gíven | to the | children of | men.

17 The dead práise not | thee, O | Lord : neither
all théy that go | down | into | silence.

18 But wé will | praise the | Lord : from this time
forth for evermóre. * | Praise | — the | Lord.

### Morning Prayer.

### PSALM CXVI. *Dilexi, quoniam.*

I AM | well | pleased : that the Lord hath héard Deliver-
the | voice | of my | prayer ;                                   ance in
                                                                 answer to
2 That he hath inclined his éar | unto | me : there- prayer.
fore will I call upon hím as | long | as I | live.

3 The snares of death cómpassed me | round a-|
bout : and the paíns of | hell gat | hold up-|on me.

4 I shall find trouble and heaviness, * and I will
call upon the Náme | of the | Lord : O Lord I be-
séech | thee de-|liver my | soul.

5 Gracious ís the | Lord and | righteous : yéa, our |
God is | merci-|ful.

6 The Lórd pre-|serveth the | simple : I was in
mísery, | and he | helped | me.

7 Turn again then unto thy rést, | O my | soul :
for the Lórd | hath re-|warded | thee.

8 And why? thou hast delívered my | soul from |
death : mine eyes from téars, * | and my | feet from |
falling.

9 I will wálk be-|fore the | Lord : ín the | land | of
the | living.

10 I believed and therefore will I speak; bút I was |
sore | troubled : I said in my háste, | "All | men are |
liars."

11 What reward shall I gíve | unto the | Lord : for all the benefits that hé hath | done | unto | me? Thanksgiving of devout service.

12 I will receive the cúp | of sal-|vation : *and cáll upon the | Name | of the | Lord.*

13 *Í will | pay my | vows : now ín the | presence of | all his | people.*

Right déar in the | sight·of the | Lord : ís the | death | of his | saints.

14 Behold O Lord, how that Í | am thy | servant : I am thy servant and the son of thine handmaid; * thóu hast | broken my | bonds in | sunder.

15 I will offer to thee the sácrifice of | thanks-|giving : *and will call upón the | Name | of the | Lord.*

16 *I will pay my vóws | unto the | Lord : ín the | sight of | all his | people.*

In the coúrts of the | Lord's | house : even in the midst of thee O Jerúsalem. * | Praise | — the | Lord.

### PSALM CXVII. *Laudate Dominum.*

O PRAISE the Lórd, | all ye | heathen : práise | — him, | all ye | nations. Praise the Lord.

2 For his merciful kindness is ever móre and | more | towards us : and the truth of the Lord endureth for éver. * | Praise | — the | Lord.

### PSALM CXVIII. *Confitemini Domino.*

O GIVE *thanks unto the Lórd, for | he is | gra-cious : becaúse his | mercy en-|dureth for | ever.* All men praise the Lord.

2 Let Israel now conféss, *that | he is | gracious : and thát his | mercy en-|dureth for | ever.*

3 Let the house of Aáron | now con-|fess : *thát his | mercy en-|dureth for | ever.*

4 Yea, let them now that féar the | Lord con-|fess :
*thát his | mercy en-|dureth for | ever.*

5 I called upón the | Lord in | trouble : and the Personal
Lórd | heard | me at | large.     trust.

6 The Lórd is | on my | side : I will not féar what |
man doeth | unto | me.

7 The Lord taketh my párt with | them that | help
me : therefore shall I sée my de-|sire up-|on mine |
enemies.

8 *It is better to trúst | in the | Lord :* than to pút
any | confid-|ence in | man.

9 *It is better to trúst | in the | Lord :* than to pút
any | confid-|ence in | princes.

10 All nations cómpassed me | round a-|bout : *but* Deliver-
*in the Náme of the | Lord will | I de-|stroy them.*     ance
     accom-
11 They kept me in on every side, they kept me in plished.
I sáy, on | every | side : *but in the Náme of the | Lord
will | I de-|stroy them.*

12 They came about me like bees, * and are extinct
even as the fíre a-|mong the | thorns : *for in the Náme
of the | Lord I | will de-|stroy them.*

13 Thou hast thrust sóre at me, that | I might |
fall : bút the | Lord | was my | help.

14 The Lord is my stréngth, | and my | song : ánd
is be-|come | my sal-|vation.

15 The voice of joy and health is in the dwéllings | Joy out of
of the | righteous : *the right hand of the Lord bring-* chasten-
*eth | mighty | things to | pass.*     ing.

16 The right hand of the Lórd | hath · the pre-|

eminence : *the right hand of the Lord bringeth* |
*mighty* | *things to* | *pass.*

17 I sháll not | die but | live : and decláre the |
works | of the | Lord.

18 The Lord hath chástened and cor-|rected | me :
but he hath not gíven me | over | unto | death.

19 Ópen me the | gates of | righteousness : that I
may go into them, ánd give | thanks | unto the | Lord. Solemn thanks-giving.

20 This is the gáte | of the | Lord : the ríghteous
shall | enter | into | it.

21 I will thánk thee for | thou hast | heard me :
and árt be-|come | my sal-|vation.

22 The same stóne which the | builders re-|fused :
is becóme the | head-stone | in the | corner.

23 Thís is the | Lord's | doing : ánd it is | marvel-
lous | in our | eyes.

24 This is the dáy which the | Lord hath | made :
we will rejoíce | and be | glad in | it.

25 Hélp me now | O | Lord : O Lórd, | send us |
now pro-|sperity.

26 Blessed be he that cometh in the Náme | of the |
Lord : we have wished you good luck, ye that arc óf
the | house | of the | Lord.

27 God is the Lórd who hath | shewed us | light :
bind the sacrifice with cords, * yea even únto the |
horns | of the | altar.

28 Thou art my Gód, and | I will | thank thee :
thóu art my | God and | I will | praise thee.

29 *O give thanks unto the Lórd, for* | *he is* | *gra-*
*cious* : *ánd his* | *mercy en-|dureth for* | *ever.*

## Ebening Prayer.

### PSALM CXIX. *Beati immaculati.*

B LESSED are those that are undefíled | in the | way :˙ and wálk in the | law | of the | Lord.

*The praises and the observance of God's law.*

2 Blessed are théy that | keep his | testimonies : and séek him | with their | whole | heart.

3 For théy who | do no | wickedness : wálk | — | in his | ways.

4 Thóu | hast | charged : that we shall díligently | keep | thy com-|mandments.

5 O that my ways were máde | so di-|rect : thát | I might | keep thy | statutes !

6 So shall I nót | be con-|founded : while I have respéct unto | all | thy com-|mandments.

7 I will thank thee wíth an un-|feigned | heart : when I shall have léarned the | judgements | of thy | righteousness.

8 Í will | keep thy | ceremonies : Ó for-|sake me | not | utterly.

### *In quo corriget?*

W HEREWITHAL shall a yoúng man | cleanse his | way : even by ruling himsélf | after | thy | word.

10 With my whole héart | have I | sought thee : O let me not go wróng | out of | thy com-|mandments.

11 Thy words have I híd with-|in my | heart : thát I | should not | sin a-|gainst thee.

12 Bléssed art | thou O | Lord : Ó | teach | me thy | statutes.

13 With my líps have | I been | telling : of áll the | judgements | of thy | mouth.

25

14 I have had as great delight in the wáy | of thy |
testimonies : ás | in all | manner of | riches.

15 I will tálk of | thy com-|mandments : and háve
re-|spect | unto thy | ways.

16 My delight shall bé | in thy | statutes : and Í
will | not for-|get thy | word.

### Retribue servo tuo.

O DO wéll | unto thy | servant : that Í may | live
and | keep thy | word.

18 Ópen | thou mine | eyes : that I may see the
wóndrous | things | of thy | law.

19 I am a stránger up-|on | earth : O híde not |
thy com-|mandments | from me.

20 My soul breaketh out for the véry | fervent
de-|sire : that it háth | alway | unto thy | judge-
ments.

21 Thóu hast re-|buked the | proud : and cursed
are théy that do | err from | thy com-|mandments.

22 O turn from me sháme | and re-|buke : fór | I
have | kept thy | testimonies.

23 Princes also did sít and | speak a-|gainst me :
but thy sérvant is | occupied | in thy | statutes.

24 For thy téstimonies are | my de-|light : ánd |
— | my | counsellors.

### Adhæsit pavimento.

MY soul cléaveth | to the | dust : O quicken
thou mé, ac-|cording | to thy | word.

26 I have acknowledged my wáys, and thou |
heardest | me : Ó | teach | me thy | statutes.

27 Make me to understand the wáy of | thy com-|

mandments : and so shall I tálk | of thy | wondrous works.

28 My soul melteth awáy for | very | heaviness: comfort thou mé ac-|cording | unto thy | word.

29 Take from mé the | way of | lying : and cause thou me to máke | much | of thy | law.

30 I have chósen the | way of | truth : and thy júdgements | have I | laid be-|fore me.

31 I have stúck | unto thy | testimonies : Ó | Lord, con-|found me | not.

32 I will run the wáy of | thy com-|mandments: whén thou hast | set my | heart at | liberty.

𝕸orning 𝕻rayer.

*Legem pone.*

TEACH me O Lord the wáy | of thy | statutes : and Í shall | keep it | unto the | end.

34 Give me understanding, and Í shall | keep thy | law : yea I shall kéep it | with my | whole | heart.

35 Make me to go in the páth of | thy com-| mandments : fór there-|in is | my de-|sire.

36 Incline my héart | unto thy | testimonies : ánd | not to | covetous-|ness.

37 O turn away mine eyes, lést they be-|hold | vanity : and qúicken thou | me | in thy | way.

38 O stablish thy wórd | in thy | servant : thát | I may | fear | thee.

39 Take away the rebúke that I | am a-|fraid of : fór thy | judgements | are | good.

40 Behold, my delíght is in | thy com-|mandments: Ó | quicken me | in thy | righteousness.

*Et veniat super me.*

LET thy loving mercy come also únto | me, O |
Lord : even thy salvátion ac-|cording | unto
thy | word.

The
praises
and the
observance
of God's
law.

42 So shall I make answer únto | my blas-|
phemers : fór my | trust is | in thy | word.

43 O take not the word of thy truth útterly ,
out of · my | mouth : fór my | hope is | in thy |
judgements.

44 So shall I álway | keep thy | law : yéa, for |
ever | and | ever.

45 And Í will | walk at | liberty : fór I | seek | thy
com-|mandments.

46 I will speak of thy testimonies also, éven
be-|fore | kings : ánd | will not | be a-|shamed.

47 And my delight shall bé in | thy com-|mand-
ments : whích | I | have | loved.

48 My hands also will I lift up unto thy commánd-
ments which | I have | loved : and my stúdy shall | be
in | thy | statutes.

*Memor esto servi tui.*

O THINK upon thy servant ás con-|cerning thy |
word : wherein thou hast cáused | me to | put
my | trust.

50 The same is my cómfort | in my | trouble : fór
thy | word hath | quickened | me.

51 The proud have had me excéedingly | in de-|
rision : yet háve I not | shrinked | from thy | law.

52 For I remembered thine everlásting | judge-
ments O | Lord : ánd | — re-|ceived | comfort.

53 I am hórri-|bly a-|fraid : for the ungódly | that
for-|sake thy | law.

54 Thy státutes have | been my | songs : ín the |
house | of my | pilgrimage.

55 I have thought upon thy Name O Lórd, in the |
night-|season : ánd | — have | kept thy | law.

56 Thís | I | had : becáuse I | kept | thy com-|
mandments.

*Portio mea, Domine.*

THÓU art my | portion O | Lord : Í have | pro-
mised to | keep thy | law.

58 I made my humble petition in thy presence wíth
my | whole | heart : O be merciful unto mé, ac-
cording | to thy | word.

59 I called mine own wáys | to re-|membrance :
and túrned my | feet | unto thy | testimonies.

60 I made haste, and prolónged | not the | time :
tó | keep | thy com-|mandments.

61 The congregations of the ungódly have | robbed |
me : but Í have | not for-|gotten thy | law.

62 At midnight I will rise to give thánks | unto |
thee : becáuse | of thy | righteous | judgements.

63 I am a companion of áll | them that | fear thee :
ánd | keep | thy com-|mandments.

64 The earth O Lord is fúll | of thy | mercy : Ó |
teach | me thy | statutes.

*Bonitatem fecisti.*

O LORD thou hast dealt gráciously | with thy |
servant : ác-|cording | unto thy | word.

66 O learn me trúe under-|standing and | know-
ledge : for Í have be-|lieved | thy com-|mandments.

67 Before I was tróubled I | went | wrong : but
nów | have I | kept thy | word.

68 Thóu art | good and | gracious : Ó | teach | me
thy | statutes.

69 The proud have imágined a | lie a-|gainst me : but
I will keep thy commándments | with my | whole | heart.

70 Their heárt is as | fat as | brawn : but my delíght
hath | been | in thy | law.

71 It is good for me that Í have | been in | trouble :
thát | I may | learn thy | statutes.

72 The law of thy mouth is déarer | unto | me:
thán | thousands of | gold and | silver.

### Ebening Prayer.

*Manus tuæ fecerunt me.*

THY hands have máde me and | fashioned | me :
  O give me understanding, that Í may | learn |
thy com-|mandments.

74 They that fear thee will be glád | when they |
see me : because I have pút my | trust | in thy |
word.

75 I know O Lórd that thy | judgements are | right:
and that thou of very fáithfulness hast | caused me | to
be | troubled.

76 O let thy merciful kíndness | be my | comfort :
accórding to thy | word | unto thy | servant.

77 O let thy loving mercies come unto mé, that | I
may | live : fór thy | law is | my de-|light.

78 Let the proud be confounded, for they go
wickedly abóut | to de-|stroy me : but I will be
óccu-|pied in | thy com-|mandments.

79 Let such as fear thee ánd have | known thy |
testimonies : bé | turned | unto | me.

80 O let my heart be sóund | in thy | statutes : thát | I be | not a-|shamed.

*Defecit anima mea.*

MY soul hath lónged for | thy sal-|vation : and I have a good hópe be-|cause | of thy | word.

82 Mine eyes long sóre | for thy | word : saying, O whén | wilt thou | comfort | me ?

83 For I am become like a bóttle | in the | smoke : yét do I | not for-|get thy | statutes.

84 How many are the dáys | of thy | servant : when wilt thou be avénged of | them that | perse-cute | me ?

85 The proud have dígged | pits for | me : whích | are not | after thy | law.

86 Áll thy com-|mandments are | true : they per-secute me fálsely; | O be | thou my | help.

87 They had almost made an end of mé up-|on | earth : bút I for-|sook not | thy com-|mandments.

88 O quicken me áfter thy | loving-|kindness : and so shall I kéep the | testimonies | of thy | mouth.

*In æternum, Domine.*

O | LORD thy | word : én-|dureth for | ever in | heaven.

90 Thy truth also remaineth from one generátion | to an-|other : thou hast laid the foundátion of the | earth and | it a-|bideth.

91 They continue this day accórding to | thine | ordinance : fór | all things | serve | thee.

92 If my delight had not béen | in thy | law : Í should have | perished | in my | trouble.

93 I will never forgét | thy com-|mandments : for
with thém | thou hast | quickened | me.

94 Í am | thine, O | save me : fór I have | sought |
thy com-|mandments.

95 The ungodly laid wait for me | to de|-stroy me :
but Í will con-|sider | thy | testimonies.

96 I see that áll things | come · to an | end : but thy
commándment | is ex-|ceeding | broad.

### *Quomodo dilexi!*

LORD what lóve have I | unto thy | law : all the
day lóng | is my | study | in it.

98 Thou through thy commandments hast made me
wíser | than mine | enemies : fór | they are | ever |
with me.

99 I have more understánding | than my | teachers :
fór thy | testimonies | are my | study.

100 I am wíser | than the | aged : becáuse I |
keep | thy com-|mandments.

101 I have refrained my feet from évery | evil |
way : thát | I may | keep thy | word.

102 I have not shrúnk | from thy | judgements :
fór | thou | teachest | me.

103 O how sweet are thy wórds | unto my | throat :
yea, swéeter than | honey | unto my | mouth.

104 Through thy commandments I gét | under-|
standing : thérefore I | hate all | evil | ways.

### Morning Prayer.

### *Lucerna pedibus meis.*

THY word is a lántern | unto my | feet : ánd a |
light | unto my | paths.

The
praises
and the
observance
of God's
law.

106 I have swórn and am | stedfastly | purposed : tó | keep thy | righteous | judgements.

107 I am troúbled a-|bove | measure : quicken me O Lórd, ac-|cording | to thy | word.

108 Let the free-will offerings of my mouth pléase | thee O | Lord : ánd | teach | me thy | judgements.

109 My soul is álway | in my | hand : yét do I | not for-|get thy | law.

110 The ungodly have laíd a | snare for | me : but yet I swérved | not from | thy com-|mandments.

111 Thy testimonies have I claimed as mine hérit-| age for | ever : and why ? they are the véry | joy | of my | heart.

112 I have applied my heart to fulfíl thy | statutes | alway : éven | un-|to the | end.

*Iniquos odio habui.*

I HATE them that imágine | evil | things : bút thy | law | do I | love.

114 Thou art mý de-|fence and | shield : ánd my | trust is | in thy | word.

115 Awáy from | me ye | wicked : I will keép the com-|mandments | of my | God.

116 O stablish me according to thy wórd, that | I may | live : and let me not be dísap-|pointed | of my | hope.

117 Hold thou me úp and I | shall be | safe : yea, my delíght shall be | ever | in thy | statutes.

118 Thou hast trodden down all them that depárt | from thy | statutes : fór they im-|agine | but de-|ceit.

119 Thou puttest away all the ungódly of the | earth like | dross : thére-|fore I | love thy | testi-monies.

26

120 My flesh trémbleth for | fear of | thee : and I
am a-|fraid | of thy | judgements.

The
praises
and the
observance
of God's
law.

*Feci judicium.*

I DEAL with the thíng that is | lawful and | right :
O give me not óver | unto | mine op-|pressors.

122 Make thou thy servant to delíght in | that·
which is | good : that the próud | do me | no |
wrong.

123 Mine eyes are wasted away with lóoking | for
thy | health : ánd for the | word | of thy | righteous-
ness.

124 O deal with thy servant according únto thy |
loving | mercy : ánd | teach | me thy | statutes.

125 I am thy servant, O gránt me | under-|standing :
thát | I may | know thy | testimonies.

126 It is time for thee Lord, to láy | to thine | hand :
fór they | have de-|stroyed thy | law.

127 For I lóve | thy com-|mandments : abóve |
gold and | precious | stone.

128 Therefore hold I stráight all | thy com-|mand-
ments : and all false wáys I | utter-|ly ab-|hor.

*Mirabilia.*

THY téstimonies are | wonder-|ful : thérefore |
doth my | soul | keep them.

130 When thy wórd | goeth | forth : it giveth light
and únder-|standing | unto the | simple.

131 I opened my móuth and drew | in my | breath :
for my delíght | was in | thy com-|mandments.

132 O look thou upon me, and be mérciful | unto |
me : as thou usest to do únto | those that | love thy |
Name.

133 Order my stéps | in thy | word : and so shall no wickedness háve dom-|inion | over | me.

134 O deliver me from the wróngful | dealings of | men : and só shall I | keep | thy com-|mandments.

135 Shew the light of thy coúntenance up-|on thy | servant : ánd | teach | me thy | statutes.

136 Mine éyes gush | out with | water : becaúse men | keep not | thy | law.

*Justus es, Domine.*

Ríghteous art | thou O | Lord : ánd | true | is thy | judgement.

138 The testimonies that thóu | hast com-|manded : áre ex-|ceeding | righteous and | true.

139 My zeal hath éven con-|sumed | me : because mine énemies | have for-|gotten thy | words.

140 Thy word is tríed | to the | uttermost : ánd thy | servant | loveth | it.

141 I am small and of nó | reput-|ation : yet do I nót for-|get | thy com-|mandments.

142 Thy righteousness is an éver-|lasting | right-eousness : ánd thy | law | is the | truth.

143 Trouble and heaviness have táken | hold up-|on me : yet is mý de-|light in | thy com-|mandments.

144 The righteousness of thy téstimonies is | ever-|lasting : O grant me únder-|standing and | I shall | live.

**Ebening Prayer.**

*Clamavi in toto corde meo.*

I Cáll with my | whole | heart : hear me O Lórd, | I will | keep thy | statutes.

146 Yea even unto thée | do I | call : hélp me and | I shall | keep thy | testimonies.

147 Early in the morning do I crý | unto | thee : for
in thý | word | is my | trust.

The
praises
and the
observance
of God's
law.

148 Mine eyes prevént the | night-|watches : that I
míght be | occupied | in thy | words.

149 Hear my voice O Lord, according únto thy |
loving-|kindness : quícken me ac-|cording as | thou
art | wont.

150 They draw nigh that of málice | persecute |
me : ánd are | far | from thy | law.

151 Be thou nígh at | hand O | Lord : for áll | thy
com-|mandments are | true.

152 As concerning thy testimonies, Í have | known
long | since : that thóu hast | grounded | them for |
ever.

### *Vide humilitatem.*

O CONSIDER mine adversity, ánd de-|liver |
me : fór I do | not for-|get thy | law.

154 Avenge thou my cáuse and de-|liver | me :
quícken me ac-|cording | to thy | word.

155 Health is fár from | the un-|godly : fór they
re-|gard | not thy | statutes.

156 Gréat is thy | mercy O | Lord : quícken | me
as | thou art | wont.

157 Many there are that troúble me and | perse-
cute | me : yet do Í not | swerve | from thy | testi-
monies.

158 It grieveth me when I sée | the trans-|gressors :
becaúse they | keep | not thy | law.

159 Consider O Lord how I lóve | thy com-|mand-
ments : O quicken me accórding | to thy | loving-|
kindness.

160 Thy word is trúe from | ever-|lasting : all the

judgements of thy ríghteousness en-|dure for | ever-|more.

*Principes persecuti sunt.*

PRINCES have persecuted mé with-|out a | cause :
but my heart stándeth in | awe | of thy | word.

162 I am as glád | of thy | word : as óne that | find-
eth | great | spoils.

163 As for lies, I háte | and ab-|hor them : bút thy |
law | do I | love.

164 Seven times a dáy | do I | praise thee : be-
caúse | of thy | righteous | judgements.

165 Great is the peace that théy have who | love
thy | law : ánd they are | not of-|fended | at it.

166 Lord I have lóoked for thy | saving | health :
and dóne | after | thy com-|mandments.

167 My sóul hath | kept thy | testimonies : ánd |
loved | them ex-|ceedingly.

168 I have képt thy com-|mandments and | testi-
monies : for áll my | ways | are be-|fore thee.

*Appropinquet deprecatio.*

LET my complaint come befóre | thee O | Lord :
give me understánding ac-|cording | to thy |
word.

170 Let my supplicátion | come be-|fore thee : de-
líver me ac-|cording | to thy | word.

171 My lips shall spéak |.of thy | praise : whén thou
hast | taught | me thy | statutes.

172 Yea, my tongue shall síng | of thy | word : for
áll | thy com-|mandments are | righteous.

173 Lét | thine hand | help me : fór I have | cho-
sen | thy com-|mandments.

174 I have longed for thy sáving | health O | Lord : The praises and the observance of God's law.
and ín thy | law is | my de-|light.

175 O let my soul líve, and | it shall | praise thee :
ánd thy | judgements | shall | help me.

176 I have gone astray like a shéep | that is | lost :
O seek thy servant, for I do nót for-|get | thy com-|
mandments.

### 𝕸orning 𝕻rayer.

## PSALM CXX. *Ad Dominum.*

WHEN I was in trouble I cálled up-|on the | Past deliverance a ground of prayer.
Lord : ánd | he | heard | me.

2 Deliver my soul O Lórd, from | lying | lips :
ánd | from · a de-|ceitful | tongue.

3 What reward shall be given * or done unto thée
thou | false | tongue : even mighty and sharp árrows *
with | hot | burning | coals.

4 Woe is me, that I am constráined to | dwell with | Evil neighbours.
Mesech : and to have my habitation a-|mong the |
tents of | Kedar.

5 My soul hath long dwélt a-|mong | them : thát
are | enemies | unto | peace.

6 I labour for peace, but when I spéak unto | them
there-|of : théy | make them | ready to | battle.

## PSALM CXXI. *Levavi oculos.*

I WILL lift up mine éyes | unto the | hills : fróm | The pilgrim's faith.
whence | cometh my | help.

2 My help cometh éven | from the | Lord : whó
hath | made | heaven and | earth.

3 He will not suffer thy fóot | to be | moved : and Divine promises.
hé that | keepeth thee | will not | sleep.

4 Behold, he that kéepeth | Isra-|el : sháll | neither |
slumber nor | sleep.

5 The Lord himsélf | is thy | keeper : the Lord is
thy defénce up-|on thy | right | hand ;
6 So that the sun shall not búrn | thee by | day :
néither the | moon | by | night.

7 The Lord shall presérve thee from | all | evil :
yea it is even hé | that shall | keep thy | soul.
8 The Lord shall preserve thy going óut and thy |
coming | in : from thís time | forth for | ever-|more.

### PSALM CXXII. *Lætatus sum.*

I WAS glad when they saíd | unto | me : "We will     Jerusalem
gó into the | house | of the | Lord."     the centre
of unity.
2 Our feet shall stánd | in thy | gates : Ó | — Je-|
rusa-|lem.
3 Jerusalem is buílt | as a | city : that ís at | unity |
in it-|self.
4 For thither the tribes go up, * even the tríbes |
of the | Lord : to testify unto Israel, * to give thánks
unto the | Name | of the | Lord.
5 For thére is the | seat of | judgement : even the
séat | of the | house of | David.

6 O pray for the peáce | of Je-|rusalem : théy shall |     Peace be
prosper that | love | thee.     upon her !
7 Péace be with-|in thy | walls : and plénteous-|ness
with-|in thy | palaces.
8 For my bréthren and com-|panions' | sakes : Í
will | wish | thee pro-|sperity.
9 Yea, because of the hóuse of the | Lord our |
God : Í will | seek to | do thee | good.

## PSALM CXXIII. *Ad te levavi oculos meos.*

UNTO thée lift I | up mine | eyes : O thóu that | dwellest | in the | heavens.    Confidence.

2 Behold even as the eyes of servants look unto the hand of their masters, * and as the eyes of a maiden unto the hánd | of her | mistress : even so our eyes wait upon the Lord our God, * untíl | he have | mercy up-|on us.

3 Have mercy upon us O Lórd, have | mercy up-| on us : fór we are | utter-|ly de-|spised.    Prayer.

4 Our soul is filled with the scornful repróof | of the | wealthy : and wíth the de-|spitefulness | of the | proud.

## PSALM CXXIV. *Nisi quia Dominus.*

IF the Lord himself had not been on our side, * nów may | Israel | say : if the Lord himself had not been on our síde, * when | men rose | up a-|gainst us;    Crisis of periL

2 They had swállowed | us up | quick : when they were so wráthful-|ly dis-|pleased | at us.

3 Yea, the wáters had | drowned | us : and the stréam had | gone | over our | soul.

4 The deep wáters | of the | proud : had góne | even | over our | soul.

5 But práised | be the | Lord : who hath not given us óver for a | prey | unto their | teeth.    Deliverance.

6 Our soul is escaped even as a bird out of the snáre | of the | fowler : the snare is bróken and | we | are de-|livered.

7 Our help standeth in the Náme | of the | Lord : whó hath | made | heaven and | earth.

## PSALM CXXV. *Qui confidunt.*

THEY that put their trust in the Lord shall be
    éven as the | mount | Sion : which may not be
remóved, but | standeth | fast for | ever.

Safety in
the Lord.

2 The hílls stand a-|bout Je-|rusalem : even so
standeth the Lord round about his people, * from thís
time | forth for | ever-|more.

3 For the rod of the ungodly cometh not into the
lót | of the | righteous : lest the righteous pút their |
hand | unto | wickedness.

4 Dó | well O | Lord : unto thóse that are | good
and | true of | heart.

Prayer for
retribu-
tion.

5 As for such as turn back únto their | own | wick-
edness : the Lord shall lead them forth with the
evil-doërs ; * but péace shall | be upon | Isra-|el.

### Ebening Prayer.

## PSALM CXXVI. *In convertendo.*

WHEN the Lord turned again the captívi-|ty of |
    Sion : then were we líke | unto | them that |
dream.

Thanks-
giving for
return
from
exile.

2 Then was our moúth | filled with | laughter : ánd
our | tongue | with | joy.

3 Then said théy a-|mong the | heathen : The Lord
hath dóne | great | things for | them.

4 Yea the Lord hath done gréat things for | us al-|
ready : whére-|of | we re-|joice.

5 Turn our captívity, | O | Lord : ás the | rivers |
in the | south.

Prayer
for its
fulfilment.

6 Théy that | sow in | tears : sháll | reap | in | joy.

27

7 He that now goeth on his way weeping, and beár-
eth | forth good | seed : shall doubtless come again
with jóy, and | bring his | sheaves | with him.

### PSALM CXXVII.  *Nisi Dominus.*

EXCEPT the Lórd | build the | house : their lá- 
bour | is but | lost that | build it.

2 Except the Lórd | keep the | city : the wátch-
man | waketh | but in | vain.

3 It is but lost labour that ye haste to rise up early
and so late take rest, * and eát the | bread of | careful-
ness : for so he gíveth | his be-|loved | sleep.

No bless-
ing with-
out the
Lord.

4 Lo children and the frúit | of the | womb : are an
heritage and gíft that | cometh | of the | Lord.

5 Liké as the arrows in the hánd | of the | giant :
even só | are the | young | children.

6 Happy is the man that hath his quíver | full of |
them : they shall not be ashamed * when they spéak
with their | enemies | in the | gate.

Children
his gift.

### PSALM CXXVIII.  *Beati omnes.*

BLESSED are all théy that | fear the | Lord :
ánd | walk | in his | ways.

2 For thou shalt eat the lábours | of thine | hands :
O well is thée, and | happy | shalt thou | be.

3 Thy wife shall bé as the | fruitful | vine : upón
the | walls | of thine | house.

4 Thy children líke the | olive-|branches : roúnd |—
a-|bout thy | table.

5 Lo thús shall the | man be | blessed : that | fear-|
eth the | Lord.

The
happiness
of the
righteous

in house
and

6 The Lord from out of Síon | shall so | bless thee : country.
that thou shalt see Jerusalem in prospérity * | all thy |
life | long.

7 Yea that thou shalt sée thy | children's | children :
ánd | peace upon | Isra-|el.

### PSALM CXXIX.    *Sæpe expugnaverunt.*

*M*ANY *a time have they fought against me fróm*  The ex-
*my* | *youth* | *up* :  máy | Israel | now | say.  perience
of Israel.

2 *Yea many a time have they vexed me fróm my* |
*youth* | *up* :  bút they have | not pre-|vailed a-|gainst
me.

3 The plowers plówed up-|on my | back :  ánd |
made | long | furrows.

4 Bút the | righteous | Lord :  hath hewn the snáres
of | the un-|godly in | pieces.

5 Let them be confoúnded and | turned | back-  Prayer for
ward :  as many as háve | evil | will at | Sion.  the over-
throw of
6 Let them be even as the grass grówing up-|on  enemies.
the | house-tops :  which withereth afóre | it be | pluck-
ed | up ;

7 Whereof the mower fílleth | not his | hand :  nei-
ther he that bíndeth | up the | sheaves his | bosom.

8 So that they who go by say not so much as, The
Lórd | prosper | you :  we wish you good lúck in the |
Name | of the | Lord.

### PSALM CXXX.    *De profundis.*

*O*UT of the deep have I cálled unto | thee O |  Prayer
Lord :  Lórd, | hear | my | voice.  and

2 O let thine éars con-|sider | well :  thé | voice
of | my com-|plaint.

3 If thou Lord wilt be extreme to márk what is | done a-|miss : O Lórd, | who | may a-|bide it?

4 Fór there is | mercy with | thee : thérefore | shalt | thou be | feared.

5 I look for the Lord; my sóul doth | wait for | him : ín his | word | is my | trust.    *trust.*

6 My soul fléeth | unto the | Lord : before the morning watch I sáy, * be-|fore the | morning | watch.

7 O Israel trust in the Lord, * for with the Lórd | there is | mercy : ánd with | him is | plenteous red-| emption.

8 And he shall redéem | Isra-|el : fróm | all | his | sins.

## PSALM CXXXI. *Domine, non est.*

LÓRD I am | not high-|minded : Í have | no | proud | looks.    Childlike humility.

2 I do not exercise mysélf in | great | matters : whích | are too | high for | me.

3 But I refrain my soul and keep it low, * like as a child that is wéaned | from his | mother : yea my soul is éven | as a | weaned | child.

4 O Israel, trúst | in the | Lord : from thís time | forth for | ever-|more.

### 𝔐orning 𝔓rayer.

## PSALM CXXXII. *Memento, Domine.*

LÓRD, re- | member | David : ánd | all | his | trouble;    The vow of David and its fulfilment.

2 How he swáre | unto the | Lord : and vowed a vow únto the Al-|mighty | God of | Jacob;

3 " I will not come within the tábernacle | of mine | house : nór | climb up | into my | bed ;

4 " I will not suffer mine eyes to sléep nor mine | eyelids to | slumber : neither the temples of my héad to | take | any | rest ;

5 " Until I find out a place for the témple | of the | Lord : an habitation fór the | mighty | God of | Jacob."

6 Lo we héard of the | same at | Ephrata : ánd | found it | in the | wood.

7 We will gó | into his | tabernacle : and fall lów on our | knees be-|fore his | footstool.

8 Arise O Lórd, | into thy | resting-place : thóu and the | ark | of thy | strength.

9 Let thy príests be | clothed with | righteousness : and lét thy | saints | sing with | joyfulness.

10 For thy sérvant | David's | sake : turn not awáy the | presence of | thine An-|ointed.

Prayer for the divine Presence.

11 The Lord hath made a faithful oáth | unto | David : ánd he | shall not | shrink | from it ;

12 " Of the frúit | of thy | body : sháll I | set up-|on thy | seat.

13 " If thy children will keep my covenant * and my téstimonies that | I shall | learn them : their children also shall sit upón thy | seat * for | ever-|more."

The permanence of the divine kingdom and of

14 For the Lord hath chosen Sion to be an habitá-tion | for him-|self : hé hath | longed | for | her.

15 " This shall bé my | rest for | ever : here will I dwell, fór I | have a de-|light there-|in.

the divine sanctuary,

16 "I will bléss her | victuals with | increase : and will sátis-|fy her | poor with | bread.

17 "I will déck her | priests with | health : and her sáints | shall re-|joice and | sing.

18 "There shall I make the hórn of | David to | flourish : I have ordaíned a | lantern for | mine An-|ointed. *through the Lord's provi-dence.*

19 "As for his enemies, I shall clóthe | them with | shame : but upon himsélf | shall his | crown | flourish."

## PSALM CXXXIII. *Ecce, quam bonum!*

BEHOLD, how good and jóyful a | thing it | is : bréthren to | dwell to-|gether in | unity! *The blessed-ness of brotherly unity.*

2 It is like the precious ointment upon the head, ⁎ that ran down unto the beard, even únto | Aaron's | beard : and went dówn to the | skirts | of his | clothing.

3 Líke as the | dew of | Hermon : which féll up-|on the | hill of | Sion.

4 For there the Lórd | promised his | blessing : ánd | life for | ever-|more.

## PSALM CXXXIV. *Ecce nunc.*

BEHÓLD now, | praise the | Lord : áll ye | ser-vants of the | Lord ; *Greeting to the watchers.*

2 Ye that by night stand in the hoúse | of the | Lord : even in the coúrts of the | house of | our | God.

3 Lift up your hánds | in the | sanctuary : and | praise | — the | Lord.

4 The Lord that máde | heaven and | earth : gíve thee | blessing | out of | Sion. *Answer.*

## PSALM CXXXV. *Laudate Nomen.*

O PRAISE the Lord, * laud ye the Náme | of the |
Lord : praise it Ó ye | servants | of the | Lord ;

2 Ye that stand in the hoúse | of the | Lord : in the
coúrts of the | house of | our | God.

3 O praise the Lórd, for the | Lord is | gracious :
O sing praises únto his | Name for | it is | lovely.

4 For why? the Lord hath chosen Jácob | unto
him-|self : and Ísrael | for his | own pos-|session.

5 For I knów that the | Lord is | great : and that
our Lórd | is a-|bove all | gods.

6 Whatsoever the Lord pleased, that did he in
héaven, | and in | earth : and in the séa, | and in | all·
deep | places.

7 He bringeth forth the clouds from the énds | of
the | world : and sendeth forth lightnings with the
rain, * bringing the | winds | out of his | treasures.

8 He smóte the | first-born of | Egypt : bóth of |
man | and | beast.

9 He hath sent tokens and wonders into the midst
of thee Ó thou | land of | Egypt : upón | Pharaoh
and | all his | servants.

10 He smóte | divers | nations : ánd | slew | mighty |
kings ;

11 Sehon king of the Amorites, * and Óg the |
king of | Basan : ánd | all the | kingdoms of | Canaan ;

12 And gave their lánd to | be an | heritage : even
an heritage únto | Isra-|el his | people.

13 Thy Name O Lórd, en-|dureth for | ever : so
doth thy memorial O Lord, from óne gener-|ation | to
an-|other.

14 For the Lórd will a-|venge his | people : ánd
be | gracious | unto his | servants.

15 As for the images of the heathen, théy are but |
silver and | gold : thé | work of | men's | hands.

16 Théy have | mouths and | speak not : éyes |
have they | but they | see not.

17 They have éars, and | yet they | hear not : nei-
ther is there ány | breath | in their | mouths.

18 They that make them are líke | unto | them :
and so are all théy that | put their | trust in | them.

19 *Praise the Lord* ye hoúse of | Isra-|el : *praise*     Praise the
*the* | *Lord* ye | house of | Aaron.     Lord.

20 *Praise the Lórd*, ye | house of | Levi : ye that
féar the | Lord, | *praise the* | *Lord*.

21 Praised be the Lórd | out of | Sion : whó |
dwelleth | at Je-|rusalem.

### Ebening Prayer.

### PSALM CXXXVI. *Confitemini.*

O GIVE thanks unto the Lórd, for | he is | gra-     Thanks-
cious : ánd his | mercy en-|dureth for | ever.     giving

2 O give thanks unto the Gód | of all | gods : *fór*
*his* | *mercy en-*|*dureth for* | *ever.*

3 O thank the Lórd | of all | lords : *fór his* | *mercy*
*en-*|*dureth for* | *ever.*

4 Who ónly | doeth great | wonders : *fór his* | *mercy*     for God's
*en-*|*dureth for* | *ever.*     works in
    creation,

5 Who by his excellent wísdom | made the | hea-
vens : *fór his* | *mercy en-*|*dureth for* | *ever.*

6 Who laid out the éarth a-|bove the | waters : *fór*
*his* | *mercy en-*|*dureth for* | *ever.*

7 Whó hath | made great | lights : *fór his* | *mercy*
*en-|dureth for* | *ever;*

8 The sún to | rule the | day : *fór his* | *mercy en-|*
*dureth for* | *ever;*

9 The moon and the stárs to | govern the | night :
*fór his* | *mercy en-|dureth for* | *ever.*

10 Who smote Égypt | with their | first-born : *fór*
*his* | *mercy en-|dureth for* | *ever;*   for the
deliver-
ance from
11 And brought out Ísrael | from a-|mong them :   Egypt,
*fór his* | *mercy en-|dureth for* | *ever;*

12 With a mighty hánd, and | stretched out | arm :
*fór his* | *mercy en-|dureth for* | *ever.*

13 Who divided the Red séa in | two | parts : *fór*
*his* | *mercy en-|dureth for* | *ever;*

14 And made Israel to gó through the | midst of |
it : *fór his* | *mercy en-|dureth for* | *ever.*

15 But as for Pharaoh and his host, he overthréw
them in the | Red | sea : *fór his* | *mercy en-|dureth for* |
*ever.*

16 Who led his péople | through the | wilderness :   for the
conquest
*fór his* | *mercy en-|dureth for* | *ever.*   of Canaan,

17 Who smóte | great | kings : *fór his* | *mercy en-|*
*dureth for* | *ever.*

18 Yea, and sléw | mighty | kings : *fór his* | *mercy*
*en-|dureth for* | *ever;*

19 Séhon | king of the | Amorites : *fór his* | *mercy*
*en-|dureth for* | *ever;*

20 And Óg the | king of | Basan : *fór his* | *mercy*
*en-|dureth for* | *ever;*

21 And gave away their lánd | for an | heritage : *fór*
*his* | *mercy en-|dureth for* | *ever;*

28

22 Even for an heritage unto Ísra-|el his | servant :
*fór his | mercy en-|dureth for | ever.*

23 Who remembered us whén we | were in | trou- for constant
ble : *fór his | mercy en-|dureth for | ever;* mercies.

24 And hath delívered us | from our | enemies : *fór
his | mercy en-|dureth for | ever.*

25 Who giveth fóod to | all | flesh : *fór his | mercy
en-|dureth for | ever.*

26 O give thanks únto the | God of | heaven : *fór* Thanks-
*his | mercy en-|dureth for | ever.* giving.

27 O give thanks únto the | Lord of | lords : *fór
his | mercy en-|dureth for | ever.*

## PSALM CXXXVII.  *Super flumina.*

BY the waters of Babylon we sát | down and|wept : The exiles
  whén we re-|membered | thee O | Sion. and their conquer-
2 As for our hárps, we | hanged them | up : upón ors.
the | trees that | are there-|in.

3 For they that led us away captive required of us
then a song, * and mélody | in our | heaviness : Síng
us | one of the | songs of | Sion.

4 How shall we síng the | Lord's | song : ín | — The
a | strange | land ? answer of the
5 If I forgét thee | O Je-|rusalem : lét my right | exiles.
hand for-|get her | cunning.

6 If I do not remember thee, * let my tongue
cleave to the róof | of my | mouth : yea, if I prefér
not Je-|rusalem * | in my | mirth.

7 Remember the children of Edom O Lord, * in Cry for

the dáy | of Je-|rusalem : how they said, Down with retribu-<br>tion.
it, dówn with it | even | to the | ground.

8 O daughter of Bábylon | wasted with | misery :
yea happy shall he be that rewardeth thée, as | thou
hast | served | us.

9 Blessed shall he bé that | taketh thy | children :
and thróweth | them a-|gainst the | stones.

## PSALM CXXXVIII. *Confitebor tibi.*

I WILL give thanks unto thee O Lórd with my | The<br>thanks-<br>giving<br>of the<br>Psalmist,<br>and
whole | heart : even before the gods will I síng |
praise | unto | thee.

2 I will worship toward thy holy temple * and
praise thy Name, because of thy lóving-|kindness and |
truth : for thou hast magnified thy Náme and thy |
Word a-|bove | all things.

3 When I called upon thée, thou | heardest | me :
and endúedst my | soul with | much | strength.

4 All the kings of the earth shall práise | thee O | of the<br>kings of<br>the earth<br>hereafter.
Lord : for they have héard the | words | of thy |
mouth.

5 Yea they shall sing in the wáys | of the | Lord :
that gréat is the | glory | of the | Lord.

6 For though the Lord be high, yet hath he respéct |
unto the | lowly : as for the proud, he behóldeth |
them a-|far | off.

7 Though I walk in the midst of trouble, yét shalt | Confi-<br>dence.
thou re-|fresh me : thou shalt stretch forth thy hand
upon the furiousness of mine énemies * and | thy
right | hand shall | save me.

8 The Lord shall make good his lóving-|kindness |

toward me : yea thy mercy O Lord endureth for
ever; * despise not then the wórks | of thine | own |
hands.

### 𝔐orning 𝔓raper.

### PSALM CXXXIX. *Domine, probasti.*

O LORD thóu hast | searched me | out : ánd
| — | known | me.       The omni-
science of
God.

Thou knowest my down-sítting and | mine up-|
rising : thou understándest my | thoughts | long be-|
fore.

2 Thou art about my páth and a-|bout my | bed :
ánd | spiest out | all my | ways.

3 For lo there is not a wórd | in my | tongue : but
thou O ·Lórd | knowest it | alto-|gether.

4 Thou hast fashioned me behínd | and be-|fore :
ánd | laid thine | hand up-|on me.

5 Such knowledge is too wónderful and | excel-
lent | for me : I cánnot at-|tain | unto | it.

6 Whither shall I gó then | from thy | Spirit : or   The omni-
whíther shall I | go then | from thy | presence ?   presence
of God.

7 If I climb up into héaven, | thou art | there : if I
go down to héll, | thou art | there | also.

8 If I take the wíngs | of the | morning : and re-
main in the úttermost | parts | of the | sea ;

9 Even there álso shall | thy hand | lead me : ánd |
thy right | hand shall | hold me.

10 If I say, Peradventure the dárkness shall |
cover | me : thén shall my | night be | turned to |
day.

11 Yea the darkness is no darkness with thee, * but

the night is as cléar | as the | day : the darkness and
líght to | thee are | both a-|likc.

12 Fór my | reins are | thine : thou hast cóvered
me | in my | mother's | womb.

His crea-
tive power.

13 I will give thanks unto thee, for I am fearfully
and wónder-|fully | made : marvellous are thy works, *
and thát my | soul | knoweth right | well.

14 My bónes are not | hid from | thee : though I
be made secretly, * and fáshioned be-|neath | in the |
earth.

15 Thine eyes did see my substance yét | being
im-|perfect : and in thy bóok were | all my | mem-
bers | written ;

16 Which dáy by | day were | fashioned : when as
yét | there was | none of | them.

17 How dear are thy counsels únto | me O | God :
O how gréat | is the | sum of | them !

18 If I tell them they are more in númber | than
the | sand : when I wáke up | I am | present with |
thee.

19 Wilt thou not sláy the | wicked O | God : de-
part from mé, ye | blood-|thirsty | men.

His
righteous
judgment.

20 For they speak unríghteously a-|gainst | thee :
and thine énemies | take thy | Name in | vain.

21 Do not I hate them O Lórd that | hate | thee :
and am not I grieved with thóse that | rise | up a-|
gainst thee ?

22 Yea I háte | them right | sore : éven as | though
they | were mine | enemies.

23 Try me O God, and seek the gróund | of my |
heart : próve me, | and ex-|amine my | thoughts.

24 Look well if there be any wáy of | wickedness |
in me : and léad me in the | way | ever-|lasting.

## PSALM CXL. *Eripe me, Domine.*

Prayer for protection against foes with-out.

DELIVER me O Lórd from the | evil | man :
and presérve me | from the | wicked | man.

2 Who imagine míschief | in their | hearts : and
stír up | strife | all the day | long.

3 They have sharpened their tóngues | like a | ser-
pent : ádder's | poison is | under their | lips.

4 Keep me O Lord from the hánds of | the un-|
godly : preserve me from the wicked men, * who are
púrposed to | over-|throw my | goings.

5 The proud have laid a snare for me, * and
spread a nét a-|broad with | cords : yéa and set |
traps | in my | way.

Con-fession and prayer.

6 I said unto the Lord, Thóu | art my | God : hear
the vóice | of my | prayers O | Lord.

7 O Lord God, thou stréngth | of my | health :
thou hast covered my héad | in the | day of | battle.

8 Let not the ungodly háve his de-|sire O | Lord :
let not his mischievous imagination prósper, | lest
they | be too | proud.

9 Let the mischief of their own lips fáll upon the |
head of | them : thát | compass | me a-|bout.

10 Let hot burning cóals | fall up-|on them : let
them be cast into the fire * and into the pit, that they
néver | rise | up a-|gain.

11 A man full of words shall not prósper up-|on
the | earth : evil shall hunt the wícked | person to |
over-|throw him.

12 Sure I am that the Lórd will a-|venge the | poor : and maintáin the | cause | of the | helpless.  Confidence.

13 The righteous also shall give thánks | unto thy | Name : and the júst shall con-|tinue | in thy | sight.


## PSALM CXLI.  *Domine, clamavi.*

LORD, I call upon thee, háste thee | unto | me :  Prayer for holiness.
and consider my voíce when I | cry | unto | thee.

2 Let my prayer be set forth in thy síght | as the | incense : and let the lifting up of my hánds | be an | evening | sacrifice.

3 Set a watch O Lórd, be-|fore my | mouth : and kéep the | door | of my | lips.

4 O let not mine heart be inclined to ány | evil | thing : let me not be occupied in ungodly works with the men that work wickedness, * lest I éat of such | things as | please | them.


5 Let the righteous ráther | smite me | friendly :  Discipline.
ánd | — re-|prove | me.

6 But let not their precious bálms | break my | head : yea I will práy | yet a-|gainst their | wickedness.

7 Let their judges be overthrówn in | stony | places : that they may héar my | words for | they are | sweet.

8 Our bones lie scáttered be-|fore the | pit : like as when one breaketh and héweth | wood up-|on the | earth.


9 But mine eyes look unto thée, O | Lord | God :  Trust.
in thee is my trúst, O | cast not | out my | soul.

10 Keep me from the snare that théy have | laid for | me : and from the tráps | of the | wicked | doers.

11 Let the ungodly fall into their ówn | nets to-| gether : ánd let | me | ever es-|cape them.

### Ebening Prayer.

PSALM CXLII. *Voce mea ad Dominum.*

I CRIED unto the Lórd | with my | voice : yea, even unto the Lórd did I | make my | supplic-| ation. The Lord the only refuge.

2 I poured oút my com-|plaints be-|fore him : ánd | shewed him | of my | trouble.

3 When my spirit was in heaviness * thóu | knewest my | path : in the way wherein I walked *have they prívily | laid a | snare for | me.

4 I looked álso upon my | right | hand : and sáw there was | no man | that would | know me.

5 I had nó place to | flee | unto : and nó man | cared | for my | soul.

6 I cried unto thée, O | Lord, and | said : Thou art my hope * and my portion ín the | land | of the | living. The sup- pliant's petitions.

7 Consíder | my com-|plaint : fór I am | brought | very | low.

8 O delíver me | from my | persecutors : fór they | are too | strong for | me.

9 Bring my soul out of prison, *that I may give thánks | unto thy | Name : which thing if thou wilt grant me, * then shall the ríghteous re-|sort | unto my | company.

## PSALM CXLIII. *Domine exaudi.*

HEAR my prayer O Lord, *and consíder | my de-|sire : hearken unto mé for thy | truth and | righteousness' | sake.   Prayer to the Lord in distress,

2 And enter not into júdgement | with thy | servant : for in thý sight shall | no man | living be | justified.

3 For the enemy hath persecuted my soul; *he hath smitten my lífe | down to the | ground : he hath laid me in the darkness, as the mén | that have | been long | dead.

4 Therefore is my spírit | vexed with-|in me : ánd my | heart with-|in me is | desolate.

5 Yet do I remember the time past; *I múse upon | all thy | works : yea I exercise mysélf in the | works | of thy | hands.

6 I stretch forth my hánds | unto | thee : my soul gaspeth unto thée | as a | thirsty | land.

7 Hear me O Lord and that soon, *for my spírit | waxeth | faint : hide not thy face from me, *lest I be like unto thém that go | down | into the | pit.   for deliverance and guidance.

8 O let me hear thy loving-kindness betimes in the morning, *for in thée | is my | trust : shew thou me the way that I should walk in, *for I lift úp my | soul | unto | thee.

9 Deliver me O Lórd, | from mine | enemies : for I flée | unto | thee to | hide me.

10 Teach me to do the thing that pleaseth thee,* for thóu | art my | God : let thy loving Spirit lead me fórth | into the | land of | righteousness.

11 Quicken me O Lórd for thy | Name's | sake :

29

and for thy righteousness' sake bríng my | soul | out
of | trouble.

12 And of thy góodness | slay mine | enemies :
and destroy all them that vex my sóul; * | for I | am
thy | servant.

### Morning Prayer.

### PSALM CXLIV. *Benedictus Dominus.*

B LÉSSED be the | Lord my | strength : who
teacheth my hands to wár, | * and my | fingers
to | fight;

2 My hope and my fortress, * my castle and de-
liverer, * my defénder in | whom I | trust : who sub-
dueth my péople | that is | under | me.

3 Lord what is man, that thou hast such respéct|
unto | him : or the son of man, that thóu | so re-|
gardest | him?

4 Man is líke a | thing of | nought : his time
pásseth a-|way | like a | shadow.

*The greatness of God and the littleness of men.*

5 Bow thy heavens O Lórd, and | come | down :
tóuch the | mountains and | they shall | smoke.

6 Cast fórth thy | lightning and | tear them :
shoot oút thine | arrows | and con-|sume them.

7 Send down thine hánd | from a-|bove : deliver
me and take me out of the great waters, * *fróm the* |
*hand of | strange | children;*

8 *Whose móuth | talketh of | vanity : and their*
*right hánd is a | right | hand of | wickedness.*

*Prayer for the revelation of God.*

9 I will sing a new sóng unto | thee O | God :
and sing praises unto thée up-|on a | ten-stringed |
lute.

*Thanksgiving.*

10 Thou hast given víctory | unto | kings : and hast delivered David thy servant fróm the | peril | of the | sword.

11 Save me, and deliver me *from the hánd of |* *strange | children : whose mouth talketh of vanity,* * *and their right hánd is a | right hand | of in- |* *iquity.*

12 That our sons may grow úp as the | young | plants : and that our daughters may be as the pólished | corners | of the | temple.　National prosperity

13 That our garners may be full and plenteous with áll | manner of | store : that our sheep may bring forth thousands and tén | thousands | in our | streets.

14 That our oxen may be strong to labour, that thére be | no de-|cay : no leading into captivity, and nó com-|plaining | in our | streets.

15 Happy are the people that áre in | such a | case : yea blessed are the people who háve the | Lord | for their | God.

　　PSALM CXLV.　*Exaltabo te, Deus.*

I WILL magnify thée, O | God my | King : and I will práise thy | Name for | ever and | ever.　Unceasing praise of God,

2 Every day will I give thánks | unto | thee : and práise thy | Name for | ever and | ever.

3 Great is the Lord and marvellous, wórthy | to be | praised : there is nó | end | of his | greatness.

4 One generation shall praise thy wórks | unto an-|other : ánd de-|clare | thy | power.

5 As for me, I will be tálking | of thy | worship : thy glóry thy | praise and | wondrous | works ;

6 So that men shall speak of the might of thy |
marvellous | acts : and I will álso | tell | of thy |
greatness.

7 The memorial of thine abundant kíndness | shall
be | shewed : and mén shall | sing | of thy | right-
eousness.

8 The Lórd is | gracious and | merciful : long- *for His gracious govern-ment of men,*
súffering, | and of | great | goodness.

9 The Lord is loving únto | every | man : and
his mércy is | over | all his | works.

10 All thy wórks | praise thee O | Lord : and
thy saínts give | thanks | unto | thee.

11 They shew the glóry | of thy | kingdom : ánd |
talk | of thy | power ;

12 That thy power, thy glory, and míghtiness |
of thy | kingdom : míght be | known | unto | men.

13 Thy kingdom is an éver-|lasting | kingdom :
and thy domínion en-|dureth through-|out all | ages.

14 The Lord uphóldeth all | such as | fall : and *for His righteous Provi-dence.*
lifteth úp all | those | that are | down.

15 The eyes of all wáit upon | thee O | Lord :
and thou gívest them their | meat in | due | season.

16 Thou ópenest | thine | hand : and fíllest | all
things | living with | plenteousness.

17 The Lord is ríghteous in | all his | ways : ánd |
holy in | all his | works.

18 The Lord is nigh unto all thém that | call up-|on
him : yea, áll such as | call up-|on him | faithfully.

19 He will fulfil the desíre of | them that | fear
him : he also will héar their | cry, | and will | help
them.

20 The Lord presérveth all | them that | love him :
but scattereth abróad | all | the un-|godly.

21 My mouth shall speak the práise | of the |
Lord : and let all flesh give thanks unto his hóly |
Name for | ever and | ever.

## PSALM CXLVI. *Lauda, anima mea.*

PRAISE the Lord O my soul;* while I líve will
I | praise the | Lord : yea as long as I have
any being, I will síng | praises | unto my | God.

The praise of God in contrast with man's weakness.

2 O put not your trust in princes, nor in ány |
child of | man : fór there is | no | help in | them.

3 For when the breath of man goeth forth he shall
turn agáin | to his | earth : and thén | all his |
thoughts | perish.

4 Blessed is he that hath the God of Jácob | for
his | help : and whose hópe is | in the | Lord his |
God ;

They that trust in Him are blessed.

5 Who made heaven and earth, * the sea, and
áll that | therein | is : whó | keepeth his | promise
for | ever ;

6 Who helpeth them to ríght that | suffer | wrong :
whó | feed-|eth the | hungry.

7 The Lord lóoseth men | out of | prison : the
Lórd giveth | sight | to the | blind.

His works of love.

8 The Lord helpeth thém | that are | fallen : the
Lórd | careth | for the | righteous.

9 The Lord careth for the strangers ;* he defendeth
the fáther-|less and | widow : as for the way of the
ungódly he | turneth it | upside | down.

10 The Lord thy God O Sion shall be Kíng for |
ever-|more : and throughóut | all | gener-|ations.

### Ebening Prayer.

PSALM CXLVII. *Laudate Dominum.*

O PRAISE the Lord, * for it is a good thing to
sing práises | unto our | God : yea a joyful and
pleasant thíng it | is | to be | thankful.

2 The Lord doth búild | up Je-|rusalem : and gather
togéther the | out-casts of | Isra-|el.

3 He healeth thóse that are | broken in | heart :
and gíveth | medicine to | heal their | sickness.

4 He telleth the númber | of the | stars : and cálleth
them | all | by their | names.

5 Great is our Lord, and gréat | is his | power : yéa
and his | wisdom | is | infinite.

6 The Lórd setteth | up the | meek : and bríngeth
the un-|godly | down to the | ground.

7 O sing unto the Lórd with | thanks-|giving : sing
praises upón the | harp | unto our | God;

8 Who covereth the heaven with clouds, * and pre-
pareth ráin | for the | earth : and maketh the grass
to grow upon the mountains, and hérb | for the | use
of | men;

9 Who giveth fódder | unto the | cattle : and feed-
eth the yóung | ravens that | call up-|on him.

10 He hath no pleasure in the stréngth | of an |
horse : neither delígheth | he in | any man's | legs.

11 But the Lord's delíght is in | them that | fear
him : and pút their | trust | in his | mercy.

Praise to
God for
His mani-
fold works
of power,
provi-
dence, and
goodness
to His
people.

12 Praise the Lórd, | O Je-|rusalem : praise | —
thy | God O | Sion.


13 For he hath made fast the bárs | of thy | gates :
ánd hath | blessed thy | children with-|in thee.

14 He maketh péace | in thy | borders : and fílleth
thee | with the | flour of | wheat.

15 He sendeth forth his commándment up-|on |
earth : and his wórd | runneth | very | swiftly.

16 He gíveth | snow like | wool : and scáttereth
the | hoar-|frost like | ashes.

17 He casteth fórth his | ice like | morsels : who is
áble | to a-|bide his | frost?

18 He sendeth out hís wórd, and | melteth | them :
he bloweth with his wínd, | and the | waters | flow.

19 He sheweth his wórd | unto | Jacob : his statutes
and órdinances | unto | Isra-|el.

20 He hath not dealt só with | any | nation : neither
have the héathen | knowledge | of his | laws.


## PSALM CXLVIII.  *Laudate Dominum.*

O PRÁISE the | Lord of | heaven : práise | —
him | in the | height.  Praise the Lord all things in heaven,

2 Praise him áll ye | angels of | his : práise | —
him, | all his | host.

3 Práise him, | sun and | moon : práise him, | all
ye | stars and | light.

4 Práise him, | all ye | heavens : and ye wáters
that | are a-|bove the | heavens.

5 Let them praise the Náme | of the | Lord : for
he spake the word and they were made; he com-
mánded, | and they | were cre-|ated.

6 He hath made them fást for | ever and | ever :
he hath given them a láw | which shall | not be |
broken.

7 Praise the Lórd up-|on | earth : yé | dragons | <sub>and on earth.</sub>
and all | deeps;

8 Fire and háil, | snow and | vapours : wínd and |
storm ful-|filling his | word;

9 Móuntains and | all | hills : frúitful | trees and |
all | cedars;

10 Béasts and | all | cattle : wórms | — and | fea-
thered | fowls;

11 Kings of the eárth and | all | people : princes
and áll | judges | of the | world;

12 Young men and maidens, *old men and children,
*praise the Náme | of the | Lord : for his Name only
is excellent, *and his práise a-|bove | heaven and |
earth.

13 He shall exalt the horn of his people; * áll his |
saints shall | praise him : even the children of Israel,
*éven the | people that | serveth | him.

## PSALM CXLIX. *Cantate Domino.*

O SING unto the Lórd a | new | song : let the <sub>Israel's</sub>
cóngreg-|ation of | saints | praise him. <sub>thanks-giving.</sub>

2 Let Israel rejóice in | him that | made him : and
let the children of Síon be | joyful | in their | King.

3 Let them praise his Náme | in the | dance : let
them sing práises unto | him with | tabret and | harp.

4 For the Lord hath pleásure | in his | people :
ánd | helpeth the | meek-|hearted.

5 Let the sáints be | joyful with | glory : lét them re-|joice | in their | beds. *The work of Israel for God.*

6 Let the praises of Gód be | in their | mouth : and a twó-edged | sword | in their | hands;

7 To be avénged | of the | heathen : ánd | to re-| buke the | people;

8 To bínd their | kings in | chains : ánd their | nobles with | links of | iron.

9 That they may be avénged of them | as it is | written : Súch | honour have | all his | saints.

### PSALM CL.   *Laudate Dominum.*

O PRAISE Gód | in his | holiness : práise him in the | firmament | of his | power. *A universal Hallelujah.*

2 Práise him in his | noble | acts : praise him ac-córding | to his | excellent | greatness.

3 Praise him in the sóund | of the | trumpet : práise him up-|on the | lute and | harp.

4 Práise him in the | cymbals and | dances : práise him up-|on the | strings and | pipe.

5 Praise him upón the | well-tuned | cymbals : práise him up-|on the | loud | cymbals.

6 Let évery thing | that hath | breath : práise | — | — the | Lord.

30